Home Spun Heritage

Home Spun Heritage

How it was/How it is

Glennys McQuade Medenwaldt

Writers Club Press

San Jose New York Lincoln Shanghai

Home Spun Heritage
How it was/How it is

Writers Club Press
an imprint of iUniverse.com, Inc.

For information address:
iUniverse.com, Inc.
5220 S 16th, Ste. 200
Lincoln, NE 68512
www.iuniverse.com

ISBN: 0-595-16576-1

Printed in the United States of America

CONTENTS

Mini-Minders from the Past

Waste not want not!

We hear about the necessity of recycling, which has become an important thing in our lives. Haven't we been doing it all of our lives? More so in the years when there wasn't ways of preserving and commercialization of things that were used and reused. Food was recycled by giving the table scraps to the cats and dogs. No dog food was purchased. What about all the recycling from milk cows? If there was an abundance of milk it would be put on the back range to turn to cottage cheese, sour milk could be used for cookies and pancakes. Cream was used for baking and churning butter and the buttermilk used for pancakes or baking. Lard left over from the previous year was cooked outside in a caldron with lye to make soap for washing clothes among other things. The wash water was used to scrub the back porch. If we used lye soap today there would probably be a lot less germs around. Bread would easily get mold on it—not to throw it away. Trim the mold and make toast, bread pudding or dressing. I wouldn't eat moldy bread now, it's for the birds. Clothes were handed down from one child to another as long as they were wearable. When there was no wear left, the best part might be cut out for a quilt patch. There was no such thing as name brands or style, I was trying to convince Aaron that a pair of jeans from a chain store for $15.00 would impress me just as much as a pair of $75.00 Dockers. If you put one beside the other I probably couldn't tell the difference. I think I lost the argument. I think recycle is a fancy word for "waste not-want not." I was brought up with that philosophy. Recently I saved a bit of something that would enhance some soup. I made the soup last week and forgot it so by now it would be good for Mr. Friskop's Science Fair if a student would care to culture, it would sure bring an A.

While I'm having my coffee and reading over this poem I was thinking of the many ways modernization has replaced the corncob.

I mourn the passage of the cob
Since mechanization has come by.
The combine strips and shatters it
Into many a tiny bit.
In days of yore, our corn was dried
upon the cob safe inside
a crib, 'til needed, then you see—
creating piles of corn and cobs, whose use could be
Soaked in kerosene to start the fire,
as a weapon, when thrown, raised someone's ire.
When stuck firmly upon a stick
it became a great backscratcher, really quick…
soaked in water at the gas station,
'Twas the bug remover, on windshields, for our nation.
And when used up, was thrown away.
A biological sound disposal, not like today.
When the plastic mesh goes bad,
more trash for the landfills quickly had.
The corn cob pipe used for centuries
are collectables now. "Antique Entries…
Open pollinated corn's cobs came in colors too,
red and white of which quite a few
were used when paper was is short supply

by rural residents such as I.
And all who had outhouses can remember when
we were GLAD, when we had COBS back then!
We used them as foot scrapers, even insulation.
Cobs were important to our nation.
They still serve in ground up bits.
Breaking up raindrops where one hits,
And keeping soil in place, erosion in check.
Cobs still are useful, by heck!
For those who never got a chance to use
a cob, the thought of them may amuse.
I truly mourn the passing of the cob…
It did a history-making job!

The Pike Press.

Winter Banes

*T*his winter has been one of the better ones most of us have seen. Wintertime usually makes us appreciate the modern conveniences we enjoy today. Meals that can be cooking and ready to serve when you get home from work, remote control starters for cars, remote control for the TV, etc. and so on through the ages life has become more enjoyable because of these inventions. Doesn't the cold weather really allure one to appreciate indoor plumbing? I had reservations about this dissertation but with a sense of humor and thinking back about it most can relate to following poem. This is from The Pittsville Press.

The Passing of the Pot

As far back in Childhood
As memory will go———
One household object greets me
That was not built for show

Beneath the bed 'twas safely anchored
Where very few could see
Yet it served the entire family
With equal privacy.

Some called the critter "Peggy"
And some "The Thunder Mug"
A few called it "Beaver"
And some the "jug".

To bring it in a evening
Was bad enough no doubt,
But heaven help the one
Who had to take it out.

Our big one was enormous
It would accommodate
A watermelon party
Composed or six or eight.

Yes, when nights were cold and stormy
It was a useful urn
And on winters mornings its icy rim
seemed to burn.

Sometimes when in a hurry
And business extra good
Each took his turn awaiting
Or done the best he could

Sometimes in the night
to our disgust and shame
We fumbled in the darkness
And slightly missed our aim.

Our special one for company
'twas decorated well.
But just the same
It had that old familiar smell.

Today this modernism
for me has done a lot
Yet in my memory
I can see this homely pot.

Author Unknown

After a couple of cups of coffee I'm glad I don't have to put on a coat, scarf and boots and make a trip outdoors. What more can I say?

P.S. If anyone should have a problem this summer I know where one can be rented for a nominal fee.

Entertainment wasn't TV or TV Games

With the approaching warm weather, robins and tulips popping out of the ground bring back childhood memories.

Having been reared in the city, there always was an ample supply of children to play with. In the neighborhood I lived in, Wahpeton's Southside, as soon as evenings were longer and warm, every child gathered on the corner, no age discrimination. Group games were played all evening, so much fun a child went home exhausted from trying to compete with the older kids.

Sides were chosen with equal ages on both, games like kick the can, pick up sticks and cricket. We played cricket with two sticks, probably a broom handle cut into a longer stick and a shorter stick. The shorter stick was placed over a hole dug in the ground and the longer stick used to see how far the shorter stick could be tossed. The further, the better.

Pick up sticks consisted of two equal sides of players. Between the two teams was a pile of tree twigs. When the leader yelled "go," you had to try and grab a stick from the pile and get it back to your team before getting caught.

There also was baseball and dodge ball. The baseball bat was probably a broomstick.

School time recess entertainment for boys was drawing a circle in the dirt to play marbles. A pouch of marbles was necessary equipment for a lad. There were the regulation-size marbles and a larger marble called "the shooter." A real lucky kid had a steely. It was so disheartening if someone won your steely.

To start the marble game, the competitors declared whether the game was for "keeps" or "funzies."

Heaven help you if a marble fell out of your pocket in school, accidentally or otherwise. It was the teacher's until school was out.

Girls were seen jumping rope. One girl was on each end of the rope and one jumped until she missed. The girls jumped rope to "salt, vinegar, mustard and pepper."

Salt was a slow turn that increased speed to pepper. It was a great accomplishment to do pepper.

Remember, "teddy bear, teddy bear turn around. Teddy bear, teddy bear touch the ground. Teddy bear, teddy bear show your shoe. Teddy bear, teddy bear 1...2...3...skidoo."

Jumping rope to teddy bear was also a real accomplishment and challenge. Whenever you missed you had to take a turn at turning the rope.

Groups of young girls also could be seen playing jacks or hopscotch.

I wonder if we had TV and computer games if we would have had these games and friendships to remember.

It's worth thinking about over that cup of coffee.

Old-Time Remedies were Simple

*O*ne of my winter pet peeves with moderating temperatures is seeing people outside wearing shorts and a sweatshirt. I can't even go out the front door to get mail without a coat or something on my head. I'd get a cold if I didn't, the kind that lasts three weeks.

This brings to mind all the old-time cold remedies for maladies. In this day, a cure for a cold would be getting a shot at the doctor's office and antibiotic prescription. Injections I don't mind, but pills—yuck! They're another story.

I don't go by the philosophy "if one pill is good, two are better." I cut a pill in half. If I find it's helping, I might take the full dose.

My vinegar and honey remedy leaflet tells to gargle with vinegar and water to ease a sore throat. Another remedy would be to rub Vicks on the soles of the feet. How about a mustard plaster, camphorated oil and the dreaded musterol? One whiff of that and your sinuses would be open the rest of the winter, not to mention the blisters if it were rubbed into the skin.

Then there was goose grease and turpentine mixture heated in with a wool cloth. The cloth, probably a piece of grandpa's longies, would be warmed by the heater and put on the chest over the goose grease turpentine remedy. The cloth had to wool to be effective.

The hot water bottle was always a necessary household item for warmth. My 6-year-old grandson Adam found my hot water bottle and wanted to know where I got my whoopee cushion? My electric heating pad is now known as "the electric whoopee cushion."

I'm scanning my 1900 Sears catalog to find the drug department. I found Dr. Hammond's internal catarrh cure, an "instant and permanent cure when located in the head. Only 50 cents a bottle. Catarrh snuffs for cold in the head, deafness and tonsillitis."

It reads, "Stop paying doctor bills and send 25 cents." For $1.50 you could buy a family medicine case with remedies. With each case they sent a homeopathic manual, a general description of diseases.

I went to my source of information about the asafetida bag. This was a source of cure. I thought it held magical powers that would discourage germs, but Ethel McIlwain informed me the potent did not have magical powers. The bag had a weed in it that was so noxious it kept people who might have germs away from you. Far away.

A good place for the asafetida bag might be at the back door at night to ward off would-be intruders. Curiosity sent me to what asafetida really is. My spelling of the word was no help, so I really searched and finally found it is a bad smelling gum resin obtained from Asiatic plants of the carrot family.

I was wondering if it was related to horseradish because one whiff of horseradish will clear your head and it has a strong odor. Not so. It's related to the mustard family.

If asafetida was available 85 years ago, would it still be out in the woods or a slough? Or maybe known by another name? Maybe a county agent or horticulturist would know. I asked our local retired pharmacist, Herman Olig, if you could still purchase musterol or camphorated oil and he assured me it is still available.

I think I'll stick with the steamer, metholatum and in desperation, half a Tylenol.

Stoves

*T*ime to wish everyone a Happy Thanksgiving and lots of family togetherness. I won't get into a sermon for Thanksgiving. I'll leave that to the more knowledgeable clergy. Instead, let's talk about how we cook the Thanksgiving meal.

It's simple today. We simply turn a few knobs and push a few buttons and the dinner starts to cook. But if I didn't have an electric stove, I would have to cut wood in pieces to fit the fire pot and fill the wood box. The firebox was a necessary kitchen appliance in years' past. All you'd have to do was start the fire to proceed with the dinner.

As I look into my 1900 Sears catalogue replica, I see coal and wood ranges. There were six different models. A beautiful black steel appliance with a choice of four or six holes was found in the pages. It had the added convenience of a warming oven and reservoir for warm water. The reservoir couldn't run dry or it would come apart. So whoever drained the last of the water had to be sure to fill it. The stoves were very ornate with nickel trim. The nickel had to be polished frequently so it would shine. It's interesting to note I don't have nickel on my electric stove today.

The better ranges had a warming shelf way back when. The even better models had a warming oven. Prices ranged for $18.70 to $26.50 for the more elaborate. Prices did not include stovepipes or cooking utensils.

Along with keeping a shiny stove, the stovepipes had to be removed and taken outside to remove the soot build-up. Failing to do so would probably cause a chimney fire. Before putting the stovepipes back—in proper order—they had to be polished with stovepipe polish, which was dull. When it was rubbed with a cloth, it looked very nice.

After all the stovepipe cleaning, needless to say, the floor had to be scrubbed. The slightest motion caused soot to fly around the kitchen like feathers.

The oven door provided a number of services. The oven would always be warm from the fire pot so all you needed to do was drop the door. It was an excellent spot for raising bread since the bread dough needed to be kept warm. You could dry socks or shoes too. It even served as an incubator for newborns that needed extra warmth. In the spring you might have brought in a piglet, wrapped it, and put it in a box to keep it warm until it had a good healthy squeal.

In the morning there would be a scramble to be first to get the best spot for dressing. The oven door was also a good foot warmer when coming in from the outside. You just pulled up a rocking chair and propped your feet on the oven door. It was very soothing in a short while.

The back burners were wonderful. A pot of soup could simmer the better part of a day to blend the flavors. You might have found a kettle of milk being kept warm for a few days to eventually turn into homemade cottage cheese. The coffeepot was always wafting a welcome to company.

Can't you just picture one of those shiny ranges in your kitchen?

I guess I'll put my coffee cup in the microwave and push a few buttons. There isn't any wood to bring in or ashes to take out with this convenience.

Rocking Chairs

*H*ave you looked really good at that old rocking chair in the corner? It isn't as pretty as the overstuffed recliner in the other corner, but when it comes to stories it could tell so many true stories of caring and of love. If you look closely, the seat is somewhat worn. The back has a pressed design at the top and spiral dowels that might cause some discomfort, and is adorned with a pieced, hand-tied quilt. The quilt probably has several pieces from dear friends that have embroidered their name on the piece, and look—there is a piece from Grandma's apron.

Can't you just see Grandpa sitting in this rocker by the old shiny hard coal heater? He is wearing bib overalls and a flannel shirt, just waiting for his Grandson to crawl on his lap. He doesn't have to wait long—the warmth of a rocking chair and Grandpa is so inviting. He might even let you listen to his pocket watch—how evenly it ticks. Grandpa surely has a story about when he was your age, how he and his dog Shep would go pocket gopher trapping with their home made wagon.

In the evening, you might remember Grandma and Grandpa each in their own rocker, with an occasional squeak, reading the Bible. Papa would pick up a Zane Gray book and Grandma would pick up the latest issue of the Dakota Farmer. She would frequently giggle as she reads "The Lazy Farmer" and then goes on to the latest recipe or pattern section.

Rocking chairs serve several purposes. They could be used for relaxing after a hard day of work— summarizing the day's activities or maybe an early evening nap, or to soothe a crying child.

Rocking chairs have come a long way from the early rocking chair. A style fitted to ladies would be a shorter chair with a rounded back, and wooden arms. A more masculine chair would be a heavy oak chair with a brown leather seat and back. There were platform rockers with the straight back, wooden arms and upholstered in velvet. They may even have an ornate design embossed on the back. Rockers without arms, just a seat and back, were more convenient for feeding babes or doing fancy work.

Over the years, you can go through several over-stuffed chairs but the old wooden rocker remains steadfast. Try it with a cup of coffee. It is inviting enough for a quick nap. After Thanksgiving dinner, pull your favorite rocker close to the stove or fireplace, sip your after dinner coffee, make your Christmas list, or start the Christmas card list.

While you are decorating for Christmas, "deck the hall"—not your spouse!

Stripping Feathers was Tedious, but Necessary

*H*ave you ever heard of the term "feather stripping?" Not talking about the feathers or plumes popular at the Malamoot Saloon back in the late 1800s. Feather stripping refers to taking feathers from the geese or ducks that were the main entree at Thanksgiving or Christmas dinners.

After the feathers were plucked from the fowl, the down feathers, the very soft feathers, were saved along with the smaller feathers, put in gunny sacks and hung out on the clothesline through most of the winter to dry-freeze dry.

Before homes had furnaces, the mode of warmth was the kitchen range and hard coal heater in the parlor. The heat would not reach the bedrooms upstairs so featherbeds were the only source of warmth. Pillows were also the recipients of the feathers.

Preparing the feathers for pillows and featherbeds was a tedious chore. The table was piled high with feathers. How do you describe stripping a feather? You had to pick up a little feather in your left hand and hold it so the tip was at the top. With your right hand you grabbed the right side of the feather and stripped it to the bottom, then turned the feather around to do the same thing to that side. All that's left is a sharp quill in your left hand. The quills were considered garbage. If the sharp quills ended up in the stuffing it proved uncomfortable.

This was a good project for a winter time consumer when the weather outside was not conductive to doing more fun things. For sure when the table was piled high with feathers and you felt a sneeze coming on, you made an exit slowly to not disturb anything. Doors were opened carefully because any small draft could create a blizzard of feathers in the kitchen or wherever you were working.

Often a few feathers strayed to the floor. One could easily lose patience trying to chase feathers with a broom. It was a lost cause. The only way to catch them was to wet the broom and that might have contained them to one spot.

The wing feathers were saved too, since they made good dusters. The wings were handy for getting in the corners. The wings were rigid buy flexible enough to serve their purpose.

Can you imagine how many stripped feathers it would take to fill a pillow?

If I remember correctly, it took about 2 1/2 pounds. Don't even ask how many it took to fill a mattress tick. Bet you're glad you can go to the store to buy a mattress all ready to put in a bed frame. I have seen a few ads lately for feather quilts. That sound inviting for a cold winter night.

I'm thinking there were a few friends who could come for the day to help and covered a lot of territory discussing, "the good ole days" over a cup of coffee and piece of cream layer cake covered with real whipped cream and toasted coconut.

I wonder what or when the "good ole days" would have meant to people in the early 1900s?

Bowl and Pitcher Thoughts

*T*hinking about things from "the Olden Days" brings to mind the bowl and pitcher set. When we think about bowl and pitcher sets we are not suggesting a bowl of cereal and a pitcher that pours milk. The old timers would tell us that these were vessels used for washing like a sponge bath. The bowl was a large basin and the pitcher was large enough at the bottom to set in the bowl tapering through the center and enlarging again for the spout. The bowl and pitcher sets were made of china with ornate trimming around the edges and handle. They were usually white, although some were more decorative. They were quite heavy and were commonly kept in the guestrooms. The pitcher would have to be taken to wherever the water was heated—the kitchen wood stove. Hopefully the last drop of water hadn't been used the night before. The unfortunate person to discover the empty pail would have to go out to fill the pail from the outdoor pump, bring it in and heat it. There was no such thing as turning open a faucet to make water flow.

The handy place to keep the set was a dry sink or a commode. For those who are not familiar with what a commode would be—they are a small dresser-like piece of furniture with sometimes a towel bar across the top. The towels were not a soft terry or velour material as we are familiar with, but a material called "crash." It came in cotton or linen and beached or unbleached—the unbleached being the most economic. The unbleached muslin was not a soft material but the more often it was washed the softer it became so by the time they got white they were worn out.

The bottom part consisted of maybe two or three drawers and a compartment with a door that was home to the china pot; also known as the chamber or "thunder" jug, a necessary piece of night equipment. There is an adage "Rich people have a canopy over their bed and poor people have a canopy under the bed." The china pot had a matching lid that was bedecked with a lovely crocheted cover. The soap was more than likely a square bar of homemade Lewis Lye soap, which was also the cleaning soap used to wash clothes, scrub floors and probably the shampoo. The soap was not a lovely perfumed piece in the shape of a shell or heart in pretty colors to offer a pleasing aroma. It was a bar of soap.

Isn't it a heart-warming thought that in the morning we can get ready for the day with a brisk shower or bask in a billowy tub of aromatic bubbles. We don't have to carry the water in, heat it, or carry it out—not to mention the "chamber chores."

Washing Machines

*T*his morning I was not happy with my automatic washing machine. I thought I could have done as well taking my clothes to the river and pounding them with, or on, a rock. I do think that is exaggerating a bit because when I think back to even having to heat water for washing I can pull in my horns. Washing clothes used to be a good half-day affair. The first machine I can remember my mom having, was a half-barrel supported by four legs. Then you put the water in it and there was a cradle with a handle and the cradle would be put on top of the clothes and worked back and forth over the clothes. A hand callousing and spine wrenching task. The clothes were wrung through a hand-cranked wringer attached to the barrel. I saw one a few years ago at a yard sale with a price tag of $400. The original price being $15.00. The cradle served another purpose if you could get away with it. Put it on the floor and crawl in and rock back and forth. Lots of fun!

When I first lived on the farm, I got in on two years of no electricity, so I got the feel of washing clothes with a washing machine run with a gas engine. The gas engine was noisy and had to be vented outside with an exhaust pipe. Not being mechanically minded, I was terrified of it. To get it started there was a foot pedal on the motor that had to be stepped down on—I guess similar to starting a motor cycle. Washing clothes was a physical thing and took care of the days' exercise. By the time you carried the wet clothes to the clothesline, chased the birds away from the line, the geese from underneath the line (it wasn't good to drop a piece of clothing on the ground) you had done a good morning work. Then you got the clothes in after they were dry and sprinkled them wet again for ironing. I think I'll have a cup of coffee and give my automatic washer a second chance.

For anyone in feel of need here is a recipe for washing clothes:

Grandm's Washday Retreet

(original spelling)

1. Bild fire in back yard to heat kettle of rain water.

2. Set tubs so smike won't blow in eyes if wind is pert.

3. Shave one hole cake of lie soap in bilin water.

4. Sort things in three piles, 1 pile white, 1 pile cullard, 1 pile work britches asnd rags.

5. Stir flour in cold water to smooth, then thin down with bilin water.

6. Rup dirty spots on board, scrub hard, then bile. Rub cullard clothes, don't bile, just rench and starch.

7. Take white things out of kettle with broom stick handle, then rench, bleu and starch.

8. Spread towels on grass, hang old rags on fence.

9. Pour rench water on flour bed, scrub porch with hot soapy water, turn tubs upside down.

10. Go put on clean dress, smooth hair with side combs, brew cup of tea, set and rest and rock a spell and count blessings.

Postscript:
Copy this and hang above your automatic washer and when you start to grumble about wash day, read it again and count your blessings.

Baby Buggy

*B*abies never go out of style. They are always soft, sweet, cuddly and if you happen to please them, may even feel obligated to smile a precious, toothless grin. A necessary piece of equipment would be a baby buggy. Years ago it was a common sight to see a mommy pushing a baby buggy in down town. Families were usually one-car families so if the head of the house needed the car for work, it was important to have a buggy so the baby would get fresh air. Baby buggies were not at all like the strollers we know today. They weren't the lovely colors or compact, collapsible to put in the car. I have two buggies. One dates back to 1900. It belonged to Albert and Anna Medenwaldt. By the time we got it, there was much-needed repair. The bottom was out of it and several side dowels. My husband disassembled it and made a beautiful buggy. I have heard that antique furniture value diminishes if it is redone, but what good is a buggy without a bottom? The buggy has dowels on the sides and an ornate bent-wood design. Large metal wheels in the back and smaller front wheels and there was an attachment for the handle to support an umbrella.

The other buggy goes back to the 40's. I still have a cloth travel-eze buggy we used for our family. This one would collapse enough to get it in the car. It was even equipped with a safety feature so if you had an active child you could harness the child and hook the harness straps to the side, thus preventing them from falling out.

I remember my mother having a wicker buggy. It was shaped like a wicker basket with a hood that would tip forward for sun protection and you might even have a net to put over the buggy to keep flies and mosquitoes from annoying the infant.

When we lived in Breckenridge, I was about 12 years old, and I had an infant sister, Gayle. My friend Phyllis Leshovsky had an infant niece, Kathleen. We would go miles around Breckenridge pushing our toothless, grinning babes looking up at us completely enjoying the ride. Phyllis had a wicker, older buggy, which was probably hers, and I had the more modern cloth travel-eze and Phyllis would say, "This buggy embarrasses me, it's so old." Phyllis most likely still has the buggy. We probably would put a bottle in their mouths and have an ice cream cone at Weiling's Confectionery and drag ourselves home.

Babies are much easier nowadays. Throw away bottles, throw away diapers, and throw away wipes, but this could all be another story.

Meeting the Elements

*T*his is really adding insult to injury when you think my story this month is about snow. When I look out at all the snow, it reminds me of stories from the "Olden Days." I wonder, when I see all of this, how did they manage back then?

It didn't matter how much snow was outside. The chores had to be done, water brought in from the pump, lamps had to be filled, coal and wood had to be brought in, and the ashes carried out. All of this was done by tunneling through snowdrifts or trudging through deep snow. Without their perseverance would we have the many items that we have today?

It really makes me appreciate the appliances and the automation of snow removal equipment now when I think of how it still could be here. I continue to have this "take out water" feeling in advance of a pending storm in case of power failure. It has happened recently in neighboring territory. That tells us we still are not infallible to Mother Nature who still commands respect.

Remember way back when Sunday was church day. No "ifs," "ands," or "buts" about it, it was not questioned about whether we would go since it was Sunday and everybody went to church. Let's take a look at how our parents and grandparents went to church during the winter.

This is Sunday morning, let's say January 10, 1924. Dad isn't going out to the nice warm garage to start the car so it's nice and warm for us. Dad is going out to the barn to harness the horses. I always thought anybody who could harness a horse must be terribly smart. All I could ever figure out about a harness was the horse collar should go around the neck and the halter would go over the head. But which end to start with to put the rest on is beyond me.

In the meantime, while Dad is preparing the sled, Mom has the stone in the oven getting warmed through to keep our feet toasty warm. Bricks or large stones were usually kept in a warm place because they would hold the heat for a long time. We didn't just flip a switch for instant heat.

Now we are going to get ready to go. We won't just put on a little jacket without anything on our head and go. It took a lot of preparation to get ready for church. The men wore two pairs of pants. Bib overalls covered their suit pants and were removed before church. A heavy sheepskin coat with a large collar was turned up to cover most of their head. The caps were wool or felt, and a muffler, or scarf as we know it, was used to keep the collar around their head.

We women aren't going to wear slacks under our heavy skirts. We wore long unmentionables covered with long black stockings. A winter bonnet was a must. We had a beautiful fur muff to slip our hands in for warmth. To me a muff is a nuisance. But on this cold day I'm sure I'll appreciate it. In pictures I've seen of women's coats they were mostly black. If you were real ritzy you'd even have a fur collar.

I guess we are ready to go now. I see the sled is up by the door. So over the river and through the woods we go because the roads we have aren't plowed out for a nice even ride.

Doesn't it sound like fun?

Some churches had barns for the horses to rest while church was in session. We have to be there at least thirty minutes before church so we can visit with friends and neighbors. If you were the janitor you would have to leave early in the morning to stoke up the big potbelly stove that usually sat in front of the church. It warmed as far as the front pew.

Now that we have arrived and the horses are in their perspective stalls, we have to keep our eyes on the clock to be sure we aren't late. If we aren't in good favor with the bell ringer or the preacher isn't in good liking, he may ring the bell on purpose so we are late. Church always starts by the janitor's watch, who was also the bell ringer. It doesn't make any difference if the president's watch was five minutes early, church started by the janitor's watch.

I'm sure glad I've got my leggings on because the floor is so cold. Oh, oh! The preacher just saw somebody checking the time of the sermon. He is going to preach 15 minutes more and sing eight verses of the next hymn instead of six.

Now that we are spiritually renewed and ready to go home, we can think about what to have for dinner. How does homemade sausage, fresh homemade bread, fresh churned butter and a jar of sauce we canned last summer sound? We finally reach home. We aren't going to just drive the car into a nice heated garage. The sled has to be unloaded by the house and then parked. The horses have to be taken into the barn and unharnessed, fed and watered. By that time dinner is ready. No, you kids can't have the horse this afternoon.

It might be a good idea to ask your grandpa or granny about going to church on a sled. They would have some interesting stories to tell of how hard the horses had to work and of tip-overs that sometimes happened.

The next time you get in your car, you might wonder, "Gee, would I really want to go if I had to go out and harness the horses and hitch them to a sleigh or buggy? Where would I put the tapes or CD player? Where would we set our pop can or coffee cup?" I think I'll have a refill and start another picture puzzle.

Raising Chickens

Spring is a good time for reflection. Thinking about new things in the manner of green grass, leaves on the trees, flower gardens and baby chickens, ducks and geese.

Oh those cute, cuddly, soft yellow baby chicks. They can capture the heart of any age—especially children. You can see the sparkle in the eyes of a child holding a chick carefully with both hands, and Grandma giving instructions on how to hold them gently, telling them to hold it to their ear so it might whisper to them.

Seeing all these baby chicks at once piques a child's curiosity. They question, "Where did we get them?" You proceed to explain that last winter we got lots of catalogs in the mail telling how we could order chickens, the prices, and what kind we'd want. Leghorns are good layers. The heavier chickens would be for the table. The chicks would be mailed to our home for a small fee.

Before the chicks arrive, there is a lot of preparation. A rule of thumb would be to order them by warm weather to save on heat. Baby chicks need a lot of TLC-24-7 you would say nowadays. The brooder house has to be scrubbed with disinfectant and well dried. The air holes need to be filled in to prevent drafts. Peat must be spread on the floor for absorption and a hoover hung in the middle to spread warmth.

You may ask, "what's a hoover?"

I guess you could describe it as a big kettle cover without the pot. It's large enough to warm lots of chicks.

You have to check the chicks at night to make sure they are warm and content. The drinking water has to be the right temperature with a pill added to keep them healthy. The feeders have to be easy for the chicks to reach. You see, there is a lot of work to get these baby chicks big enough to lay eggs.

A good thing to think about when ordering chickens is to order a few extra ones for a hungry fox or mink. Perhaps some day you may look at your flock, and for some unexplained reason, it seems a few are missing. When you question this, your 4-year-old son offers the explanation that "he and Spot don't like chickens so we put them in the hog feeder."

How come you're not smiling Dad?

Despite all the work and TLC that goes with raising chickens, there is nothing like a home-grown chicken that's grilled, baked, fried, smoked, or put in soup.

I think it's time for another cup of coffee!

Flowers

I have been reflecting on what a neat town we have here in Hankinson. As you drive through the street you can't help but notice the shrubbery and flowers in their ornate pots or set against the foundation of a home.

I have no talent when it comes to arranging a flowerbed decoratively or a bouquet attractively. I have an admiration for people who can do it. My houseplants mostly are ivy. They don't blossom anyway but do tend to flourish. Of course, the plants that should bloom don't, they are just green.

My garden also has much to be desired. I have weeded, watered, threatened, and to no avail. The onions are one inch across, there are four beets, and the potatoes have bugs. The best cure for potato bugs is a block of wood and a hammer. I may give up gardening.

I think this is what our town would say if it could communicate.

"Hello, I am a friend of yours. You know me well. You, my people take good care of me. From a distance, you see the towering church spires built by your ancestors. You, the present generation, have cared and kept them beautiful along with carrying on the Sunday morning worship traditions. How their bells peal out welcoming one and all to 'Come, let us worship God together, whatever your faith.'

'The trees are lovely this time of year. Their stately trunks have branches of leaves that invite everyone to come and rest in the shade for a while. Look at the colorful homes—high homes, squatty homes, homes with fireplaces, homes old with age—each with a different story to tell. Can you imagine the stories these homes would tell?'

'Let's look at the flower gardens you have adorned me with. I just marvel at the art and beauty of each bloom as it is complemented by another.'

'These are just some of the things that make me proud to be a part of you. I hope we can stay friends forever.'

'I am your city. Hankinson."

I think I will have a cup of coffee and sit on my yard swing under a beautiful shade tree. Would somebody tell me why Four O'clocks are blooming at 9 a.m., and the Morning Glories are blooming in the afternoon?

Goose Eggs

*M*any years ago, this was the time of year when you were thinking about getting the goose and duck eggs set. A good setting hen was the hatchery. We collected the eggs every other day.

The first goose eggs were marked so that if you happened to have a cluck they could be set first. The eggs had to be turned often while they were in storage. The eggs had to be taken from the goose because, after laying what she thought was an ample supply, she would start the warming procedure. Thus you would have goslings before the weather was conducive to the little fluffy creatures.

Once you had a sufficient collection of eggs it was time to hope the hens would be ready to set—sit—set. I'll go back with set. If you had Leghorn chickens, they weren't gifted with the ability or patience for setting. They were more the egg layer variety of chicken.

Well, if you didn't have a cluck you would begin calling friends, relatives or neighbors to see if they had a breed of chicken that was taking up nest space by just setting and not producing. You could borrow and return the hen, or our best bet was to buy one because the hen may meet with its demise while borrowed.

When bringing your setters home, you had to be very careful not to break their setting spell. When you got them home you had already prepared your wooden boxes with straw. If you weren't sure one would set, you had to put some wooden eggs in to fool the hen, or you had to cover them for a few days to make sure they were going to tend to their intended business before putting the real eggs under them.

Finally, you had to decide the hens knew exactly what you wanted them to do so you could place the eggs under them. A hen can only accommodate four goose eggs, where a goose can cover up to 12 eggs. The next thing was to go to the calendar and mark off 28 days.

The week before the hatching would commence, you had to go out and candle the eggs. This procedure was done with a flashlight behind the egg to see if it was dark, assuring there was life in the egg. Another way was to use a kettle of warm water. Gentle wiggling by the egg, you could know if there was life inside. This was mysterious to the children. The clear eggs would be discarded far away.

Sometimes if you held the egg to your ear you could hear a faint "peeping." After another week, you had to patiently watch for the first sign of a picked egg and wait to bring in the first gosling. The goslings had to be taken away from the setter; otherwise she might think her job was done before it was time and abandon the nest.

Now that you have a box of cute little fluffy balls of feathers, they had to be fed. You had to don your canvas gloves and go out and cut nettle. I had never had the experience of cutting nettle, only by mistake with bare hands. They say that once nettle is cut the itch is gone. The nettle is cut fine and mixed with oatmeal, and is quite delectable if you're a goose.

This might be the easy way out, but if I wanted to raise geese today, I would get my hatchery fliers out, pour a cup of coffee and lift the telephone receiver to place my order that would be delivered straight to my door.

Deciphering Recipes

I like to bake and I had been looking for a recipe for a pineapple upside down cake. I had scanned the recipe books and to no avail. What to do? Let's see what the 1936 Watkins cookbook has. If you have one it's on page 103. I was also hunting for a gingerbread recipe. While I'm scanning this recipe book to see what other goodies I could find, I noticed that ingredients have changed over the years. For instance, a bread recipe calls for yeast foam, or compressed yeast or a cake of yeast. If I remember, yeast was a hard square about 2 Inches and it took some time to dissolve it.

Looking at the cake section, the recipes are requiring butter, lard, and thick sour cream. These items today are frowned upon.

The thing that really caught my attention was that there were no degrees marked for baking. A slow, moderate, or hot oven, for so many minutes, was suggested. I also noted a "quick" oven. How hot is a quick oven? How to tell how hot your oven is, I found in the back of the book. Slow oven 250 to 350 degrees; moderate oven is 350 to 400 degrees, and hot oven is 400 to 450 degrees. If you have no oven thermometer, set a pan sprinkled with flour in the oven and if it becomes a delicate brown in 5 minutes, the oven is slow. If the flour turns a medium golden brown in 5 minutes, the oven is moderate. If the flour turns a deep, dark brown in 5 minutes the oven is hot. My patience just wouldn't allow me to put up with that.

I note that the cookie recipes call for butter or lard. I'm sure that at the time this book was printed the farmers had their own fresh churned butter and home rendered lard. The measurements also caught my attention, such as about 3 cups, batter not too thick, thin batter. A chunk of butter off the butter dish was 1/2 cup. A capful of vanilla, was a teaspoon.

Recently my grandson walked in the house and headed right to the cookie jar. To his amazement, it was empty. "Grandma, this is the first time you haven't had cookies!" Now that laid a little guilt trip on me. On another occasion, I had a cake baked and frosted for church. I had forgotten to red flag it as a no, no. Here he comes from the kitchen with an ample size piece of cake. I am sure I wouldn't have said "no" anyway.

Here is a tidbit I found in a cookbook.

Be sorry for people,
whoever they are,
who live in a house,
where there is no cookie jar!

How about an empty cookie jar? I found a recipe for bars so I will set my oven for 350F and bake something to have with coffee.

Grocery Stores Today have really Evolved from Earlier Counterparts

*R*ecently I was talking on the telephone with my older brother, Archie McQuade. Our conversation turned to groceries and about how he was a grocery bagger at the Red Owl Store in Wahpeton in the late 30s.

We were talking about how we go to the store today and everything is packaged. A person picks what they need, puts it in a grocery cart, proceeds to the check out counter and pays for the groceries.

Some of the things we discussed I remember from those days, like when you went into the store there weren't any shopping carts. A person just gave their list to the "behind the counter clerk." It might consist of sugar, which came in a 100-pound bag. If a shopper wanted a 5-pound or 10 pound bag, it would be scooped into a smaller bag and weighed. Coffee came in 100-pound bags, also, and would be ground right in the store. A person's 1 or 2 pounds was weighed and bagged then.

Cookies were in a large box at 15 cents a pound, and were weighed and bagged.

Butter came in a large tub and 1 pound of it would be cut out for 5 cents a pound.

Bacon was a rasher or slab and kept in the cooler counter. A pound would be cut off and put back in the cooler. Hamburger was in a big tray in the cooler. The meat counter manager took out the tray and weighed the desired amount and then returned the tray to the cooler.

Farmers brought their produce to the store and traded it for groceries.

Eggs were put in a grocery bag, not egg cartons. I remember arriving home several times with a wet bag with at least one squished egg. Eggs were candled in the store, too. Some stores also bought cream and had equipment to test for butter fat content. The cream and egg profits bought the groceries.

Bananas were hung from a stock and the number wanted was taken off by the clerk. Peanut butter came in a large container and could be purchased by the pound. The oil always surfaced and had to be stirred before a person could make a sandwich.

Poultry would even be butchered in the back of the store. The head was wrapped in paper and feet were tied together. A sign in the window read, "Fresh New York Style Chickens."

I don't remember the pickle barrel, only what I've seen on TV westerns.

Wouldn't the FDA have had a hay day back then?! Something from our century to think about over a cup of coffee.

Churning

I enjoy making homemade bread and hamburger buns. I even tried whole wheat bread that turned out all right. Jim calls sometimes and requests homemade hamburger buns. A bowl of fresh churned butter would be nice to put on my fresh homemade bread. In this day and age, it's probably not a good idea. Oh, well!

We lived on the edge of town when I was a child, which enabled us to have a cow. After the morning milking chores were done, my mom would put the milk in pans so the cream would rise to the top and then skim it off. She saved the cream in a 2-quart jar, which then acted as the churn.

Somehow the jar fit my hands just right and was a good job for a teenager. I would sit by the radio and shake the jar to "One O'clock Jump," "In the Mood" or "Chattanooga Choo Choo." The later song was a better tune to encourage butter.

Later on, we got a gallon jar with a wooden paddle inside and turned it by a crank. It did lessen the chore and improved the beat to the aforementioned tunes.

After I moved to the farm, I was astonished to see a churn that resembled a half-barrel on four legs with a large paddle inside. This apparatus made a two quart jar seem quite primitive. I was equally amazed at seeing two gallons of cream being poured into the churn. Churning this amount of cream was a long, hard task and required "manpower." There was a plugged hole at the base of the churn to drain the buttermilk. When Paul was small he would stick his finger in the hole and lick the butter. This amount of cream left a good chunk of butter and lots of buttermilk for cookies or pancakes.

"Waste not, want not."

Finishing the butter was up to the woman of the house. The buttermilk was drained off and then the butter had salt worked into it, about one or two handfuls. Then clear water was poured over it and then that water was worked out of the butter. The finished product was put in a bowl. I'd put some attractive mounds on an ornate plate that made me not want to cut into it. A butter paddle was a necessary implement in accomplishing this feat.

The more sour the cream, the better the buttermilk tasted.

Sometimes in the spring, you could detect a strange taste in the butter. This taste was attributed to the cows being on grass.

It's time to have a slice of homemade bread, my store-bought low cholesterol margarine and homemade jelly. There was a time when Sure-Jell was 25 cents a package. Wouldn't a glass of chilled, fresh buttermilk be good instead of a cup of coffee?

Grandma's Trunk Treasures

Spring is the time of year for house cleaning. Good house cleaning—like getting the corners, curtains, cupboards and the junk drawer.

My younger sister, Gayle, loves to paint and decorate. She is much better at it than I am. She called one evening and announced she would come and redo my dining room. All right! I called in Jim and Aaron to move furniture so all would be ready for her. While painting she would say, "Isn't this fun?"

My reply, "No, it's not!"

Moving back to normal was fun. My dining room, which was a kaleidoscope of color, was transformed into two colors plus one item I wouldn't give up. It was taxing to have to give up my varied colors, but I needed somebody to say, "This has to go!"

Now that my dining room is done, let's go up to the attic and see what we can find up there. Come along. We carefully walk up the creaking stairs. Oh, look over there! It's the old gas lamp. Quite dusty and no mantels on it, but with a little TLC it would still work.

Over there is Grandma's baby buggy. It has two large wheels at the back while the front wheels are smaller. The handle even has a place for a sun umbrella. The sides of the basket are wooden dowels with a bentwood scroll design. I can picture a baby in it covered with a white satin coverlet trimmed with handmade lace and a pillow to match. The buggy is equipped with springs beneath it that would make for a comfy ride.

Look! Over there, it's Grandma's platform rocker, quite elite with a velvet cushion and back. It has a lovely, carved wood design at the top. Can't you just see her sitting on it, humming a tune to comfort a child?

There's the trunk. Let's look inside. Oh, here's Grandma's wedding dress. You say, "black wedding dress?" Yes. It's adorned with black lace trim and tiny buttons. She must have been a beautiful bride. This must have been Dad's baptismal dress with a petticoat and bonnet to match. So tiny and delicate, but very long. The lace and fine ribbon along with tiny rosebuds make it look so elegant. It appears to have been handmade and has yellowed with age.

Let's see what's in this box. It's Grandma's locket with here and Grandpa's picture. It's oval shaped with a diamond in it. It is so precious.

Here's another box. Grandpa's watch and fob. I can picture him sitting on the front porch in his wooden rocker and taking out his watch to see if it's time for the mail train to come through or time for Grandma to have lunch on the table.

Grandma's photo album sure is heavy. We could spend hours going through it, trying to guess who is in each picture. Who could this be running the thrashing rig, or team of horses pulling the bundle wagons? Here is the family picture. Everyone is sitting so straight and looking very stern.

When we turn the page, again Grandma and Grandpa's wedding picture is seen. This is a different setting. Grandpa is sitting in a lovely wicker chair while Grandma is standing beside him in her black wedding dress. Let's take the album downstairs and wander through it.

Oh my, there goes a mouse! Help!

We can wash down the dust with a cup of coffee. I wonder what our kids will be amazed at in our trunk of precious memories. Will they be wondering why Grandpa is sitting and Grandma is standing?

Sunbonnets

What has happened to the sunbonnet? Sun bonnets were a must for women who worked in the hayfield or in the vegetable or flower gardens, or any type of outdoor work that required protection from the sun. It just wasn't lady-like to have dark skin in those days. A blustery winter day would be a good day to make the summer supply of bonnets. There would be a sunbonnet for every day type work, and a special bonnet for going to clean the cemetery or maybe a special one for the church picnic. Sunbonnets were made of pretty calicos, perhaps a flowered material of yardage left over from a dress. Or in the days when chicken feed was sold in figured feed bags, there would be enough for a bonnet from one bag of feed. If you bought lots of feed, three feed bags would make a dress of a simple pattern or 6 feed bags would make a quilt top. It didn't make the head of the house to popular if he bought feed and there wasn't a qualified number of matching sacks for one of the aforementioned projects. The sunbonnet pattern consists of two main pattern parts. The brim, which sticks out quite a way in front of the face for good protection, and was long to the back of the head. The brim would be cut double so there would be a lining and it would be sewed from front to back at about 1-1/2 inch intervals across to enable cardboard strips to be inserted to keep the brim stiff. The back was cut large enough to be gathered onto the brim, and a seam binding sewed across the back at the neck level to run a string through to gather for a comfortable fit. The back part was long enough to cover the neck, so I've been told, to keep the flies off the neck. Oh, yes, we must have bias tape to sew around the whole bonnet, of course, to match the fabric. Then there are ties to make a lovely bow in the back.

Being it is summer time, I won't be sewing any bonnets or making any hay. Maybe the garden could use some attention.

Bonnets required special care after washing. They had to be starched and ironed to look neat. The cardboard strips had to be removed before laundering. When the ironing was done, the cardboard strips would be carefully replaced and basted along the edge to hold them in place.

After a cup of coffee, or two, we are ready to go to the hayfield or garden—I can't forget my sunbonnet!

Quilts

Quilting is an age-old necessity and quilts never go out of style, especially in the north where winters can be quite severe. Years ago, you couldn't just go to the dry goods store and buy a wool bat. You took the bat from an old quilt and/or wool from sheared sheep and took it to the woolen mills and trade if for a fresh wool bat, at a reduced price. This would be done early in the fall so that by the time winter set in, it would be ready for the "quilting bee" parties.

A quilt frame was a necessary piece of equipment for making a firm, lovely, cuddly quilt. Some quilt frames were without legs and needed to lie on chairs and some had legs making it an easier job for rolling the quilt. There were flannel strips adhered to two sides of the frame. The bottom side of the quilt basted to the two sides, then the bat filler laid on and then the beautiful pieced top laid on and then the tying could begin. Of course, there must be a pot of coffee and fresh rolls for a break, or two, in the day.

I noticed that some of the old quilt top patterns from years ago have been revived. The lone star pattern, the log cabin, trip around the world, wedding ring, and just plain blocks can be arranged attractively. Sewing quilt blocks into an attractive pattern can take a lot of patience. Once finished, a beautiful product results. Nice enough for a coverlet. Each quilt with the matching colors must have whatever is used to tie it in colors to match or stand out.

Upon completion of the tying, the quilt had to be hemmed by hand.

When the quilt is taken from the frame, four of the young, single gals are rounded up and each takes a corner of the quilt in their hand and a cat is put in the middle of the quilt. Each single gal would flip the corner to keep the cat away because wherever the cat jumped out would indicate that she would be the next to be married.

While we have our second cup of coffee we can be thinking about who we will have at our next "quilting bee"—don't forget your thimble!

Kerosene Jug and Egg Beater

*R*ecently, I was at a flea market at Detroit Lakes visiting my sister, Gayle. We saw so many things that reminded us of our childhood. One of the first things we saw was a gallon kerosene jug. Gayle reminded me how she had to go to the store and get a gallon of kerosene for 15 cents, and bring it home to fill the kerosene jug that would be turned upside down carefully, so as not to spill, and put it in the receptacle at the end of the stove. Kerosene did not heat as hot as gas or electricity. For instance, it took a good hour to cook a kettle of potatoes. Sometimes, if the burner were accidentally turned to high, the smoke would start pouring from the chimney and blacken the kettles. This necessitated a good cleaner and some elbow grease to get them clean again.

The other thing that fascinated me was the eggbeater. Remember getting the eggbeater out of the drawer and trying to whip eggs and invariably the wheel would jam after about two turns and you would have to put it in reverse to get it to work properly? And then maybe proceed two or four rounds before you had to repeat the reverse process? This could become quite aggravating. While I'm having a second cup of coffee, I'm thinking about before angel food cake mixes. The cracked eggs were save to make angel food cake (much frowned upon now). The whites had to be whisked with a special wire whisk. The eggbeater didn't incorporate enough air to make a nice froth. Later, when electricity made its appearance, the electric mixer replaced the eggbeater making batter mixing so simple. When I watch gourmet cooks on TV, with their electric blenders, and the dough mixers, it makes the eggbeater look like a Volkswagen beside a Cadillac. Then, too, if you can't find your eggbeater, it might be in the toy box. It made a good motor boat.

If I need a cake, instead of a bowl, a big spoon, and retrieving all of the items that go into a cake, I'll just get out a cake mix and whip it with the electric mixer and open a box of ready-made frosting for the icing.

I guess the best use for the eggbeater would be to make an egg beater macramé plant holder.

Old Crocks

*H*ow many times have you been in your basement and walked by that old crock? Well, they aren't lovely to look at or delightful to hold. Years ago they were very necessary in food preservation. Crocks came in many sizes: 1 quart, 2, 5, 10 and 20 gallons. These are sizes I'm familiar with. There may be more. Most crocks are gray, and sometimes the size was printed on the side in blue. If you have a crock with "Red Wing" on it, you can expect a good price for it. Of course, it must not have any cracks or chips.

You might ask how these were important to food preservation? In the days before electricity, it was necessary to preserve meat products in a crock and pour lard over the meat and put it in the cellar. Roasted pork ribs, sausage, meatballs, and other meat could be kept well into the summer with this method. This would be so handy in the summer time when the thrashing crews would visit, or if it was too hot to start the range. A trip to the cellar would provide a hearty meal.

When the winter butchering was being planned a big sow must be one of the main things to have in order to have at least a 20-gallon crock of lard. Rendering a 20-gallon crock of lard was not a pleasant chore. It would be done, if at all possible, in the summer kitchen. The aroma of rendered lard is not the most pleasant, but once done, it provided for the year's supply of lard. The lard would be stored in the smaller crocks.

Another kind of crock was the brown bean crock, and was also used for jelly. These had a cover and a wire handle for carrying. A 5-gallon crock would be used for straining plum juice and the juice would be cooked into jelly and put into the brown crocks and waxed and it kept well through the winter. It was a delightful compliment to a slice of homemade bread and fresh churned butter. Doing the jelly-making chore for several years has not left me with a good feeling for plums.

Do you remember in the country school, the big water crock with a spigot? Often the chemicals left a brown ring around the inside of the crock.

I know it's much frowned upon nowadays but is there anything better than fried potatoes in rendered lard? Yes, I still render a bit of lard. I like it for piecrust and greasing bread pans and cookie pans.

I'm wondering about the use of a 20-gallon crock, what were those contraptions called that required copper tubing? Or was that a barrel? Keg?

While I think about it, I'll have a slice of bread, but with strawberry jelly and a cup of coffee.

The Charivari (chivaree)

I'm wondering if the young people today would know what a "charivari" is? Well, it might be equivalent to a "kegger" after a wedding. Webster defines a charivari as "a mock serenade, as to newly weds, made by blowing toy horns, beating on pans, etc.," and also called chivaree. Chivarees were frequently held in the late 40s, or early 50s, and even now there might be an occasional chivaree.

Let's say a young man and lady had their wedding, but neglected to provide friends and relatives with a dance, they might be chivareed.

A group of uninvited guests, male and female, would secretly descend on the bride and groom after the wedding. First, a meeting was held to decide where and when to have the chivaree. A captain was chosen. The event had to be late in the evening after dark because it should be unknown to the couple. The cars would have the lights off so the participants could sneak up to the house without being detected. Everyone brought their own noise makers such as guns, kettles, spoons to pound with, plow shares, or anything that would make lots of noise.

On signal by the captain, the noise would begin, and continued until the couple appeared at the door. If the surprised couple didn't present enough money, one of them could be held hostage. When finally enough was given, but wait a minute! The captain says it isn't enough for a "kegger," the banging and shooting commenced. Ah! Finally enough money was scrounged up so that the hostage was released and friends departed wishing the newly weds good luck and best wishes—they might even be invited to join the party. The chivareers would then go to someone else's home and have their party, play cards, and have a pot luck lunch.

Not all's well that ends well. Sometimes a gun would misfire and there would be a hole shot through eaves troughs, or maybe a few chickens would be found on the ground that had been disturbed from their roost in the trees.

Chivarees have been replaced by the wedding dance. The Chivaree was an act of good will and friendship.

Food for Thought

*P*reserving food has at one time in my life been a hobby, addiction or necessity. The time has come when it isn't necessary to can what once was required to provide proper nutrition for my growing family.

Somehow the urge to can is still compelling. I can't resist the cherries in the store. But I have some left over from last year. However, temptation spurred me on. Now I can't wait for peaches. I used to can four crates of peaches. Today, one crate is sufficient, considering the stash left from last year.

I've been pondering on the canning season. As hot as it is today, I'm glad there is nothing ready to can. That brings to mind how they preserved food years ago. If we go back to the early Indians, history tells us they dried meat and other foods that kept well. Wouldn't they have enjoyed an electric dehydrator then?

Last summer I was at Fort Abraham Lincoln, at Mandan. As we looked at the different Indian mounds, I discovered what must have been the locker plant. There was an apparatus that gave me the impression it was used for drying meat.

The next thing that comes to mind is canning. Can you imagine hauling in wood and keeping a canner going in the kitchen for three hours when the outside temperature was 95 degrees? That happened not too long ago. Women couldn't use a fan or air conditioner to keep the house cool and comfy because homes didn't have electricity; thus no plug-ins.

There used to be a building on the farm called the "summer kitchen." This was really a lifesaver. The washing could be done there along with the canning and baking bread, keeping the regular kitchen clean and not so hot. The summer kitchen was equipped with a wood stove, gas engine washing machine, and the canning equipment. It wouldn't be classed as a step saver, because there was still a lot of footwork back to the kitchen, but it was a real luxury.

Before electricity was common on the farm; refrigeration was accomplished with a "cream cooler." If you milked cows and separated, the way to keep the cream cool was in the cooler—not the fridge. The cream cooler was a large round wooden vat with a pipe running into it from a windmill that pumped in cold water. On the other side was a pipe leading into the stock tank so there was no wasted water. The household milk and butter would be put in appropriate containers and kept there. Before preparing a meal, all these necessities would be brought to the house. After the meal, they were taken back to the cooler.

Before deep freezes were common in the home, one way of preserving meat was cooking it well done and packing the meat in a crock. Rendered lard was poured on top to cover it. This would be so handy when the threshing crews came. Meatballs, ribs, and sausage could be done this way. Home cured ham was a summer treat. The hams would be soaked in salt water strong enough to float an egg. In two weeks, the water had to be changed and fresh salt water prepared. The hams were then soaked another three or four weeks. Following this procedure, the hams had to be smoked for about four to six weeks. They were stored in a barrel with oats packed around them or hung in the basement.

I never did develop a taste for home cured ham. I compare it to salting a piece of shoe leather and chewing on it. Having been reared in the city, my palate was unaccustomed to such a delicacy. But "when in Rome, do as the Romans do." My boys do get a yearning for home cured ham and have to make some every few years.

It's getting to be suppertime. I'm glad I don't have to jog down to the cooler for milk and butter. I would probably bring one thing and forget the second. I'm also glad not to head to the basement to dig meatballs out of the lard. I can go to the fridge in one or two short steps, then go to the deep freezer and grab a piece of meat. After dinner, I put the leftovers in the fridge, toss the dishes in the dishwasher and settle down for a nap.

I do enjoy going out to the farm to help Laurie with the garden vegetables. When they are ready, give me a call and put the coffee on. I'll be there.

Bread is the Salt of Life

I have a thing about convenience foods, for instance foods you can microwave in minutes. If you are pressed for time and need something in a hurry they are O.K. but I'll have a piece of toast from homemade bread. One of the more modern conveniences on the market is the automatic bread maker. This item has not been high on my wish list. I enjoy making my bread from scratch because I have the time. A piece of homemade bread toast at bedtime is like a sleeping pill for me.

I was wondering one day (for lack of something better to do) when bread making started, so I did some research in the encyclopedia. I found out that bread is the most widely eaten food. The most popular is white bread. There are quick breads, muffins, baking powder biscuits and flat breads including matzah, tortilla, and crisp bread; most enjoyed by Latin Americans.

Prehistoric people made flat bread by mixing grain meal with water and baking it on rocks that were heated. Bread has been baked since 2600 BC. Until the 1900s, most bread was baked at home. Bakeries were established in early American colonies as early as 1640.

When you compare the cost of store bread to what the home made variety is, and compare the cost of yeast and flour, it's still worth the effort.

Bread can be frozen and when taken from the freezer doesn't have to be peeled, cooked, baked, or canned. It's ready for toast, jelly, peanut butter, bread pudding, dressing, or lunchmeat. It ranks right up with the versatility of the potato, and yet is more convenient.

Butchering

"*T*he time of year is descending upon us where we think of giving "thanks" for all the goodness bestowed upon us; and after Thanksgiving holiday we start to think of butchering. The delicacies that come from the result of this tedious procedure could be known by a better title than butchering.

Sausage making time isn't quite appropriate because it doesn't quite cover all the aspects of the procedure. Ah ha, I've got it! "Beer Drinking Time" would cover all aspects because any time there is a lull "it's beer time," and hopefully when the time comes to season the meat it won't be two salt to 1 pepper or is it 1 salt and 2 pepper? Maybe that's why we have recipes. The reason for beer is it helps cut the grease. Yah, yah. Let's talk about doing it the hard way. First, we have to set a date because three or four families will get together at each other's homes and it usually takes a week from start to finish. After setting the date we have to be sure Taunta Emma is free to come and help. The first thing she did was make a batch of fudge. Now this being my first experience with butchering, I couldn't see fudge being synonymous with butchering! But, again it helps cut the grease, smell and taste, now that, I could go along with! This is something completely new to me. As far as I knew, meat came from a meat market.

Let's get going. We have to do the beef the day before to allow proper cooling. Save the tail for me. Oxtail makes the best soup. The next day we have to get up early and get the water hot for scalding the hogs. They could be skinned but we have to have rinds that had to be scraped well, cleaned and cooked for the potato sausage. Oh, yes, everything on the hog is used except the squeal and I mean everything, including intestines, which we will discuss later. By the way, the water was carried from the well. If you toted a five-gallon slop pail in each hand it took fewer trips. We aren't going to do just one hog, we are going to do three or four because we have to have a years supply of lard. Nothing like home rendered lard for piecrust. We weren't worried about cholesterol then. Back to things at hand. After the hogs have been done, the heads have to be cleaned and sawed apart and don't forget to save the ears. Papa's favorite, and the brains. It takes the brains from about four hogs to make a meal; fried with onions and butter—now that was a breakfast worth getting up for. The rest of the head meat is used for blood sausage and liver sausage. Now blood sausage—just the name is enough to nauseate you! The feet we will put away in a cool place for another day. We don't have time for that today because they have to be scalded and scraped and the toenails taken off and then we might as well throw the tail in with that. While the hogs are cooling, let's cut the beef that was cooled from the night before. We'll cut some steaks and trim the bones for hamburger and save the soup bones for canning later. How about one inch steaks, shoulder steaks or maybe one shoulder into roasts. Rib steaks are always a favorite. We aren't too fond of ribs so lets trim most of them for hamburger. There was no deep freeze so we couldn't wrap too many for freezing. We could rent a locker so freezer space is limited. We have to cook the liver so it can cool for the liver sausage and cook the head meat. We have to save the sirloins and porterhouse steaks. Gee, I wish a cow had two tenderloins, and two hearts. One tail is enough. If you ever sat on a milk stool to milk you could get the tail in your mouth. It was always good thinking to keep your mouth shut during milking.

Let's get back to cutting steaks—round steaks could be cut for frying, maybe a rolled roast with dressing, or run through the tenderizer for a quick summer meal. We need a couple rump roasts too, and some T-bones.

Now the hogs are cooled so we will make some shoulder roasts or shoulder steaks, lots of pork chops. We have to trim the fat from them, good for rendering. The lief lard has to be kept separate because when you fry that it splatters more. Ah, the bacon, nice and meaty for curing and smoking. Let's make one or two hams into ham steaks and have a few for curing and the ham hocks for boiling meat. Pork ribs and sauerkraut always make a good hearty meal. Now that we've got the meat all trimmed we are ready to grind it into big wooden tubs. While some are doing that we better get the meat ready for the potato sausage. Hopefully, we haven't forgotten to soak the casings the night before, with frequent water changing. We will need lots, like fifty pounds of peeled potatoes, and someone to grate the potatoes, a mean to the fingers job. Cooked ground rinds and we have had to render a bit of lard to have nice brown cracklings. Salt and pepper is the only seasoning we need for this. We will just smack and taste to see if it's enough. A little extra salt won't hurt. It will cook out when we cook it after it's stuffed. Now that made me thirsty. Time out for a brew, or a piece of fudge.

OK, back to work. Let's get this stuffed. We need four volunteers. One person to turn the stuffer, one to hold the casing. Remember that it has to be stuffed loosely because it expands when it is cooked and could possibly break the casing. One person needs to hold the sausage and one does the tying. While you do that, I'll prepare the fixin's for the blood sausage. We need to have caught blood from the hog, at least one gallon, it has to have the veins gathered and taken out and this must be done immediately. I only know two procedures. One is to add salt and stir it for a while. The other is to stir the warm blood with the hand until all the veins gather in a ball. I prefer the latter method. Now then, we need a loaf of dry bread soaked in water and squeezed dry. Raisins soaked until soft and drained. Some people prefer other ingredients in blood sausage. Some enjoy it sweet, we do. Some prefer it without sugar. It takes a lot of sugar if you like it sweet because the raisins tend to make it sour. We like a touch of cinnamon and salt and pepper. If they are done stuffing the potato sausage, they can start mixing this all together. Add the head meat, now to sample it for seasoning. Everybody gathers round. It seems all of a sudden that everyone has found something to do that just can't be left. OK, you win. We'll just fry some and then sample. Sighs of relief all over. Same procedure for stuffing potato sausage.

Now for liver sausage. We need head meat, brine that the head meat was cooked in and the liver, also onions. We will grind it all together, put the brine salt and pepper and again same stuffing procedure. Break time before the big job. We have the pork and beef ground so now it's seasoning time. I would guess one hundred fifty pounds. We will need two cups of salt, one cup of pepper and some tender quick. We don't want it too fatty because it won't keep as well. Again, people have their own favorite recipe of different spices. It takes a while to get the spices mixed in so we can start frying samples. The opinions vary from too much salt to not enough pepper, but a rule of thumb we go by is you have to taste the pepper. After numerous samples have been sampled, it tends to make one thirsty, and so, before stuffing the sausage we have a quick fudge break. No fudge for me, it's too sweet. I need something liquid. OK, back to work now. We need four people for stuffing again.

Only the beef sausage has to be stuffed firmer. As soon as the sausage is stuffed it must be hung immediately, otherwise, if it lies packed together a liquid forms that could cause it to poison. Hurray! The big job done.

We aren't done yet by a long shot. The messy utensils, tubs, and saws have to be washed and put carefully away for next year. Over the rest of the week there will be a twenty-gallon crock of lard to render. That is a days work in itself. You have to watch each kettle carefully so it doesn't stick and not to overcook it. The crackling golden brown cracklings are just about right. It has to be strained into containers—you must be careful not to burn yourself. After the lard has cooled and set, each jar has to be well covered to prevent varmints from getting into it in storage.

The next day maybe we will can meatballs from some of the hamburger we saved, and we have to package some hamburger for everyone to take home and sample. The next day or so we might can soup. The soup bones are cooked in a big canner until the meat falls off the bones. The meat is packed in jars and the brine comes to the top of the sterilized jars. Salt is added to each jar. Lids and rings go on and jars are put back into the canner for three hours.

The casings have to be kept warm while stuffing or they will cause breaks. Speaking of casings, I did mention we would discuss that later and later it is. Not really a pleasant subject but it goes with the territory. Intestine casings were used mostly for the blood sausage and potato sausage. The first thing was to empty them—'nuff said! Then you needed a pitcher and lots of hot water. The intestine would be put in the pitcher of hot water and the end turned back and as you emptied the pitcher the intestine would turn inside out. Sounds simple doesn't it? After that was accomplished, each casing would have to be stripped with a big hairpin. I tried but I couldn't do it. To slimy I guess. Then soaked in vinegar water. Now that wasn't hard was it? I'm sure there are a lot of stories that could be told about things I don't know about like using the stomachs and the different preparations.

When we are wrapping meat for the deep freeze, now we always mark special packages for summer time grilling. We put the deer meat with pork for the smoked sausage and wrap all the ground beef for hamburger. There is never enough hamburger. Having worked in a locker plant for a few years, and wrapping as much as 200 packages of hamburger a day, hamburgers are my least favorite food so when I take out a package of hamburger, I'm desperate! Next week will be somebody else's turn for the party. When it's all done, it's so nice to be able to go to the deep freeze and take out the next day's menu or for unexpected company.

A Winter Fashion Show

(Part 1)

I am having the good fortune of reviewing a 1936-37 Montgomery Ward winter catalog, so I thought it would be fun to have a fashion show from that era. It is cold and snowy out so what better to do? Let's get started.

The first page is showing ladies hosiery. They come in many different qualities. Some of the styles include sheer chiffon, endurance chiffon, and service weight. A two thread quality that wears like a four thread quality at 95 cents a pair or two pairs for $1.85. Full fashion silks are priced at 39 cents a pair. The most expensive pairs are $1.29. Mercerized lisles, cotton stockings are 27 cents a pair. Every day cotton stockings were two pairs for 25 cents.

The next section is winter coats. One page is shown in color, not the vibrant colors we have today. We see browns, rust, gray, black, and plaids. The finest furless collar coat with a back center gore was $12.98. The fabrics are mostly wool. Here is a three-piece wardrobe: a jacket, skirt and overcoat, all to match in wool nubby tweed. The coat has a fur collar of silky dyed fox fur and all for the price of $19.98. Oh, my goodness! Here are wool coats for $6.79. Now we get into the precious furs. An all wool coat with gorgeous natural Russian Red Fox collar for $39.98. The fur collars are quite ample and come way down on the shoulders. Some of the coats are showing the straight lines with large buttons, single or double breasted and are all shown about mid-calf to ankle length. Oh, here is a muff for a dollar; wolf dyed Manchurian dog fur. The cheapest coat is shown as without fur, yet warm at $4.98. The best long fur coat is a beaver dyed coney priced at $49.98, or a seal dyed at $39.98.

Let's look at the hats. There are so many styles from which to choose. The felt masculine look with a feather or a bit of veil priced at $1.29. Here are some styles on this page that are called turbans, derbys, pancake crowns, visor brims all priced from $1.00 to $1.98. Most are shown with a rhinestone pin, ribbon, feathers, and veils were real classy.

What's new in dresses? Skirts that flare at the bottom, or are pleated; mid-calf or ankle length—embroidery, pleats, lace and bows. The more expensive dress is $4.98 in celenese acetate crepe or satin rayon. Pleated lacy bodices with ruffled collars seemed to be the style. Here are some long dresses. We would call formal wear velvet—unheard of at the price of $7.98, a lace trim satin at $4.98. Here are the cotton housedresses for 49 cents. Checkered or flowered tub fast percale, what we call a jump suit, is referred to as overalls at 94 cents.

Let's look at some of the nightwear. Steam pre-shrunk, non-sagging, hold their shape pajamas—flannel, cotton and rayon—many styles at 95 cents. The best flannel was $1.39. The best quality long-sleeved gown was 95 cents or two for $1.85. Hand embroidered cotton gowns are shown at 37 to 79 cents.

As I look at the dual control foundation garments—well, there just aren't words to describe them—maybe torture! No panty hose or panty girdles were featured.

The shoes are shown with lots of straps, some laces, and quite decorated with bows and rhinestones. Dull suede with patent trim was popular. The large square heels are called Cuban heels. The heels shown are mostly high, 2-1/2 inches. The price range is from $1.77 to $3.19. I remember getting bunny slippers for Christmas, 69 cents a pair, and Three Little Pigs slippers for 35 cents a pair.

I so well remember the two button overshoes. Not good for water puddles, but only 89 cents a pair. A pair lavished with fur $1.89.

Oh, mommies! Diapers 49 cents a dozen standard quality. Diaper covers, all rubber 9 cents. You could buy a whole baby layette for $4.45, 35 pieces. The best grade of baby shoes was 74 cents. Baby undershirts, 23 cents. Little boy coveralls, sizes 2-8 are 55 cents, 95 cents for a better quality. Bib overalls, $1.19 for the best and 55 cents for a lesser quality. No belt jeans shown until size 8.

Looking at men's suits—all wool worsted suit with two pants, $17.50. They featured either single or double-breasted, plain or belted back. A lot of pin stripes and checks as well as plain colored patterns to choose from. The lapels were quite wide and cuffed trousers. Now we get into work clothes. A pair of bib overalls was 93 cents for the better quality. Ten ounce denim waist band overall $1.00. A blanket lined jacket, $1.59. Think about wearing a pure virgin wool union suit, it says warmest of all at $4.45, but then there is also the winter weight at 89 cents. How about a dress shirt for $1.29 in stripes, checks or plain? Ninety-four cents for a sanforized shrunk shirt. There is a wilt proof collar shirt for 94 cents. Flannel shirts of 1/3 wool and 2/3 cotton for strength, with a double back are $1.79. Then there were the chambrays for 65 cents, and 44 cents. The Rockford socks like you make the toy stuffed monkeys from were three pairs for 37 cents. Rayon and cotton men's socks were three pair for 28 cents. If you wanted pure silk, 45 cents a pair. Dress shoes, it seemed anything goes. Wing tip, square or round toes at $3.85 a pair. This book even features spats. Thrifty at 59 cents and wool box cloth for $1.65. How about a pair of 8 inch work boots for $2.79, or $1.89. Here is a special work shoe regular $3.00, on sale for $2.00.

Wouldn't it be fun to make out an order? I guess in those days, $1.00 was just as hard to come by as $10.00 now.

While you have coffee, you could get out your latest catalog and compare prices, at least on the standard items.

Shopping for Furniture

(Part 2)

*L*et's go furniture and household shopping in a 1936 catalog.

Looking at bedding I see supreme quality muslin sheets at $1.15, deluxe percale at $.39, pillow cases at 71 cents, and bedspreads of rayon and cotton for $1.88, or rich rayon and taffeta for $2.89. Can you imagine the best quality bath towels at 23 cents each, wash cloths at 6 for 28 cents? Oil cloth for a table cover was 27 cents a yard, or 39 cents for a square 54 inches. Material for a quilt was from 22 cents to 11 cents a yard. Sheer curtains were $2.95. For a better quality kitchen curtain, deluxe 59 cents a pair, jumbo priscillas 106" wide, $1.69. Two pleated drapes, $1.24 and up to 5 pleats for $4.79. Try and buy a tie back for that amount now. Here's a finest quality davenport and chair $99.95. An angora hair set for $64.75. A chair and ottoman cost $19.95. Here is a card table and four chairs for $5.95. I recently paid $30.00 for a card table. Three piece bedroom sets for $29.85, economy, to $72.95 for a deluxe. The average for an 8-piece dining room group about $60.00, made of walnut. Kitchen cabinets with a flour bin and a breadbox were from $44.95, down to $19.95. Here's an 8 tube, all-electric radio console for $48.95. Oh, we need a new wringer washer, regular family size for $31.95 or with a gasoline engine, $54.75. Here is a deluxe wood-burning range with a double warming oven and a water reservoir with a handy tip-up faucet. Here's a kerosene range, high-powered wick type burners for $37.95. Then we need a refrigerator, a full 6.33 cubic foot capacity, $97.50.

Now we come to the china. A 76-piece, matched table service for $8.98, complete 32-piece dinner set, 18-piece glass set, and 26-piece silverware set. I don't see any electric percolators. Drip coffee makers from 49 to 98 cents. How about some prices on ordinary kitchen items. Pressure cookers, $11.29, canner, $1.10, aluminum roaster, 67 cents, kraut cutter, 97 cents, food grinders, $4.39—no food processors. Ice cream freezer, $3.49, copper boiler, $3.49, kerosene bracket and lamp, $1.45, designer kerosene lamp, $2.59, kerosene lantern, $1.15, wicks extra 10 cents. Some items for the medicine chest—toothpaste, some of the brands, Dr. Lyons, Pebeco, Mickey Mouse, Colgate, Listerine, Dr. West's, all at about 26 cents a tube. Toothbrushes were 47 to 9 cents. Sloan's Liniment was 29 cents; Mentholatum was 23 or 42 cents.

Maybe we should have some 1847 Rogers Brothers silver service—a 30 piece set for $29.95. My Rogers Brothers sterling silver service was $90.00 in 1948. I wonder what the value would be now?

The car needs a new battery. A 128-ampere, hour capacity is $10.25. Power grip tires, 6 ply, $7.40 or four ply, $5.80.

I haven't found any microwaves, TV's, dishwashers, automatic washers, dryers, deep freezes, self-defrosting refrigerators, air conditioners, water beds, automatic bread makers, clock radios, battery operated clocks, or furnaces.

I didn't find any culottes or shorts, pretty T's or sweatshirts, or slacks for ladies. I'm sure they would have been rated as unlady-like.

The Antique Doll

*I*n my day, say the late 1800s—I was as loved by little girls as are the dolls of today. I have a china head, so please handle me with tender, loving care.

The rest of me is cotton material, and I am stuffed with straw. I wear several petticoats with beautiful hand-embroidered lace that is now very fragile from the years.

My dress is a heavy material. It is very hot in the summer, with the heavy petticoats. My dresses have always been brown or dark blue, because they masked the soil.

My dress has a gathered skirt. It is gathered onto a fitted bodice that boasts lovely buttons and lace. The sleeves are very puffy from the elbow to the shoulder, and they are fitted from the elbow to the wrist. They are called leg-of-mutton sleeves. My shoes are black high-tops made of something similar to oilcloth.

My hair is quite matted from the years. I have lovely blue eyes and they are still sparkly. I don't do a lot of things like the dolls of today, like crawl or walk, drink from a bottle or cry "mama." I just enjoy my place in the glass case and watch what is going on, and wonder what being a doll today would be like?

Fireplace Warmth

*I*n recent decades, fireplaces have once again become popular. Fireplaces have become a thing of beauty; constructed of stones artistically arranged, or of brick in a colorful design.

Remember seeing pictures of pilgrim women doing their cooking over a kettle hanging on a tripod or doing their baking in a fireplace? Can you imagine yourself cooking in this manner today?

Wouldn't a pilgrim woman gaze in awe at our beautiful electric gas, or electric ranges, not to mention the convenient microwaves? I'm sure even a gas or charcoal grill would have been a joy to ease the hardships of household cooking.

I'm straying from the fireplace idea. The fireplace of years ago would have grandfather's picture above it, very stern looking with a handle bar mustache and a neatly brushed beard.

His white shirt had a very white and starched stand-up collar (likely boiled in Lewis Lye soap), and his vest was adorned with a beautiful and mysterious watch pocket with a chain and watch fob. The picture is in an oval frame that reminds you of one of our modern day conveniences.

Can't you just picture a big, friendly calico cat all curled up in front of the fireplace on a brightly hand braided rug, watching the warm blaze and listening to the crackling wood?

On the mantle might be an ornate candelabrum…and a beautiful bouquet of colorful fresh garden flowers. Nearby there would be two rocking chairs—his and hers. I can imagine a friendly discussion of who should get up and put the next log on the fire.

Our fireplace today would feature a large picture of scenery, perhaps a forest or an ocean scene with vast ships and billowy clouds, surrounded by a lovely carved oak frame. The mantel might be adorned with graduation pictures or family photographs or some lovely family heirlooms. Rather than a cat on a braided rug in front of the fireplace, there would be a soft plush rug with a footstool with a needlepoint, embroidery top.

At Christmas time, fireplaces are adorned with garlands of evergreen boughs emitting pine scent throughout the house. On the mantle would be a manger scene.

Think of the miles of stockings that are strung across fireplace mantels throughout the years just waiting to be filled.

Stockings of hand knitted wool might be replaced by some of the present day panty hose—more practical for lots of gifts.

There is something romantic about the flickering flames. They say that wood warms you twice—once when you cut it and again when you burn it.

I haven't experienced the laborious part, but I have enjoyed the warmth of burning logs, and I have toted more than a few.

Kerosene Lamps

Garage and auction sales are wonderful places to find items of fascination, useful or not. I feel defeated if I go home with nothing. There is always the chance you will meet an old friend you haven't seen for a long time. It takes time to catch up on the old days.

It is fun to watch items being auctioned off that I have been familiar with over the years, such as an old kerosene lamp for instance. You may feel they have smelly kerosene or smoked chimneys, however, they have to be an improvement over the candle.

Kerosene lamps were a lot of work at the height of their use. They had to be filled with kerosene and the chimneys, which easily became sooty if the wick was turned too high, had to be washed with soap water, rinsed and polished until they were shiny. The wicks needed trimming and occasionally had to be replaced. I also learned, through painful experience, you don't touch a chimney after extinguishing the flame.

You might think a kerosene lamp had a glass base or that the chimney and wick were very plain. But as I scan my 1900 Sears catalog, I note three pages of lamps, some of which were very ornate. The banquet lamp stood 25 inches tall, and had a 12-inch globe and 13 inch bowl. It rested on a gold plated stand, beautifully hand painted in floral decor. The best one sold for $6.95.

The reading lamp sold for $2, while the kitchen reflector lamp was only 75 cents. The hanging lamp with extensions that lowered it to 61 inches had two prices, the economical lamp was $2.48 while the more ornate with prisms sold for $8.25.

The next time you go to an auction sale, take a look at this part of history.

Today a kerosene lamp would be a decorative item with lovely smelling fuel, or you might have a lamp for your fish house or camper.

My son, Jim, has a fascination for kerosene lamps. He feels each lamp has a personality and story. You might have a kerosene lamp on hand for an emergency should the power go off for an extended period of time. Lamps haven't outlived their usefulness.

I really am appreciating the light switch. I wonder why someone hasn't invented a pull down chandelier to make changing light bulbs easier? Something to ponder over a cup of coffee. While wondering about the prices of the original lamps, take note of what these items are going for at an auction.

The Separator

Do you remember the old cream separator? This subject is not dear to my heart. There are many women who share my (lack of) sentiment on this subject.

I was a transplant from the city to the farm. When the subject of washing the separator arose, it may as well have been a portfolio or a room divider, anything that needed separating.

I recently found a DeLaval Handy Reference Yearbook from 1940 promoting the cream separator at a cost of $24.75. There are many interesting tidbits in that book. Did you know 1 gallon of skim milk is equal to 1-1/2 pounds of cottage cheese, 1-1/2 pounds of lean beef or 10 eggs?

Every farmer should have at least one good milk cow for home use. An interesting weather fact: "Harken to a cricket chirping. Count the number of chirps in 14 seconds. This number added to 40 gives you the temperature in degrees Fahrenheit.

The book also gives directions on how to wash the separator in five minutes. To me, the 10-step procedure looks longer than washing by hand.

My orientation to washing the separator was not impressive. Oh, it looked simple enough when looking at it—a milk bowl, two spouts (one for cream and one for milk) and a float bowl. But there was this heavy bowl that contained about 18 disks that had to be hand washed. These disks were put on a special hanger. On occasion, they would slip off the contraption. They would then have to be put on the bowl post by hand (taking more time).

A requirement was hot water. It was always a hope you might get out and get it done before someone was yelling "M-O-M-M-Y I'm hungry"…

"where's my shoes?" By the time you put out a bowl of cereal and found shoes, the water had cooled.

In the summer it was necessary to get it washed before the heat of the day and soured what didn't wash through. During winter, it would be frozen if you didn't get it washed out soon after milking was completed.

The hand crank separator was a boon to the dairy farmer. It was better than hand skimming cream from the milk pans or the continuous centrifugal separator, which I found in my Handy Reference Book was invented in 1878.

The electric separator was a real blessing over the hand crank. It kept the speed even, which was needed for a good cream test. After cranking the separator by hand for so many years you could almost feel embarrassed watching the milk run through it with no effort. You could even grab a pail of skim milk and slop the hogs or feed calves while the other pail was filling.

The bulk milk tanks that followed finally relieved the tedious chore of daily separator washing. One of my first fears was having to put the thing together. If not done properly, the cream might come out someplace other than where it was supposed to. Or, if everything wasn't properly placed in order, the milk would begin spewing out an improper place and create a mess.

I salute the dedicated women and children, and a few men, who had patiently done this daily chore over the years. There is a consoling part to this. Nobody else begged to do this. It would be a quite time. The most noise might come from a clucking chicken. Needless to say, if you needed peace and quiet, you'd just retreat to the milk room with a pail of water. It was a good time for reflecting. After you were done, you'd grab a cup of coffee.

Sandwich with Lard was Standard Not Long Ago

*T*his is the time of year when we see big, orange school buses arriving in town with students. Thinking back to years ago, the mode of transportation was very different. Ask your grandparents. They could tell stories of how they walked miles to school in the winter's cold, and having to crawl through or over fences carrying their books in one hand and a syrup pail containing dinner in the other.

Some families were fortunate enough to have a horse or even a horse drawn buggy. In the winter, lunch might be frozen when you finally arrived at school, so lunch pails ere lined up by the hard coal heater.

I had heard about some old-time conveyances of transportation to school. Irma (Gaedcke) Tucker, Osseo, Minn., who attended Belford country school, reminded me of the peanut wagon. I thought that was worth some research. That led to the caboose, which entailed more research.

One mode of transportation was a topless buggy, which was used for spring and fall use. Winter transportation was a binder frame with skis and a box sturdy enough to hold several people. This was driven by Bruno Medenwaldt, which is the best I can do to find out about the "peanut wagon."

There was another contrivance called "the caboose" built by August Pankow. Seven or eight children could ride inside and six on top. I wonder if that would pass inspection codes today? Of course, it didn't go without mishap. Margaret Steffens related she fell off and broke her arm not once, but twice. Hearsay is that this one horse vehicle was difficult for the horse to pull because it was quite heavy and when going downhill, the caboose would almost overtake the horse. Rudolph Pankow was the chauffeur and one stop would be to pick up the Krump children.

This might be cause for argument, but I've heard Medenwaldt's had the fastest horse. Probably a good argument to that would be that it had a lighter load. This makes me wonder if there wasn't some racing done to prove a point.

What is the lesser means of transportation? Riding a nice and shiny, warm school bus for an hour or a horse and buggy for a half-hour?

For lunch, the hot lunch program would be a great improvement over the syrup pail that probably included bread with lard, a piece of sausage and an apple from the apple barrel. It maybe didn't contain all the vitamins and minerals for the daily requirements, but when you were hungry it was delicious.

I guess I'll have a sandwich for lunch today, but it won't have lard on it.

Rubber Soles Prolonged Life
of Shoes Years Back

*D*o you remember way back many years ago when getting clothes was so special?

I could hardly wait to display my new array. The usual attire for school was two dresses, home made, and a Sunday dress.

There may have been a few aprons to change off during the week. And the girls wore long black or brown stockings to school.

Girls from a more well to do family had white stockings. I longed to be able to wear white stockings. However, when I was on the way to school, I couldn't go around any water puddle—I walked through them to see how deep they were. By the time I got to school I was wet to the knees. Maybe that's why I wasn't allowed white stockings.

Remember how the black patent leather shoes had to have Vaseline put on them to keep from cracking?

A relative sent me this account she remembered form her childhood:

"When we were kids and the sole of our shoe came unstitched, we would have to sling our foot out in front in order to walk. It got me to thinking about how I used to wear my shoes out so quickly. I remember I could wear a hole in the bottom of my shoe, then showed it to Daddy and he would cut a piece of shirt cardboard to fit inside my shoe.

"I wore that cardboard in my shoe until he found time to go to the 'Five and Dime.' There, he bought a pair of rubber soles that were much too big for my shoes and he would glue them on the bottom of my shoes. In the morning before school, Daddy would take out his pocketknife and trim around both shoes and I was ready to hit the road once again."

The same thing happened at our house, only when I saw a hole starting to show I'd think, "Oh, goody! I'll get a new pair of shoes!"

I was reminded of the rubber soles we could put on. They might have stayed glued for two weeks, thus prolonging the life of the shoes, but the disappointment of not getting new shoes until the old pair was not repairable was so disheartening.

While I'm sipping my coffee, I'm thinking I should toss mine in the washer and freshen them—something you couldn't do with patent leather shoes.

Pumps and Windmills

When you drive around, whether it be town or country, you are most apt to see a windmill or a pump, although not in use extensively nowadays, you will likely see them as decorative yard decorations. I have even seen the old cream separator as a yard decoration with the milk bowl filled with soil and lovely flowers blooming. The old hand pump might be situated on a piece of wood or cement and flowers growing around it.

Years ago, the windmill and pump were necessary items on the farm and even some city homes had a cistern pump. The cistern was a cement pit located near the house and collected the rainwater from the roof by means of eaves troughs. The rainwater was used mainly for cleaning jobs, doing dishes, washing clothes, and oh, so nice, for washing hair. I can remember my mom collecting rainwater for the purpose of Saturday shampoos for us girls. After the shampoo she would make several perfect long finger curls, and after the tedious procedure we had to sit still until they were dry. We had heavy hair and it took eons, so it seemed, before the curls would dry. Having to sit still that long was pure torture.

With a cistern pump in the house it eased the chore of carrying water from the well, which was used for drinking and cooking.

The windmill you would see on the farmstead, or it might be out in the pasture. It was mainly used to water the cattle and horses. The windmill was a tall, steel structure with a wheel made of blades and it was driven by the wind. If the wind didn't blow, you might have to pump the water manually.

It was usually necessary to leave a container of water by the pump to "prime the pump" because the leathers would dry out and it wasn't a good idea to forget. Occasionally the leathers in the pump would become worn and need to be replaced.

The rainwater would make the homemade Lewis Lye soap really foam. Once in a while, the cistern would go dry and then it would be a good time to clean it.

Aren't you glad you can just go out to the barn and flip a switch and have instant water? I'm glad I can go to the kitchen sink, open the faucet and have instant water for my coffee and not have to prime the pump.

Think of the Stories our Porches could Tell

*R*ecently there was a song out pertaining to "Everyone should have a front porch like they did way back when."

When you drive around town have you ever noticed front porches on homes? Somehow a front porch adds warmth to a home. Porches are plain, open, screened in, windowed, or maybe contain just a railing.

Porches can serve several purposes. For one, then can be a play area for children. Picture small girls playing house pretending one side is the kitchen with leaves and stones for fine china and a cardboard box for the kitchen table. Little boys, on the other hand, might find a place for a pretend farm. They may have a box for the barn, and a block of wood with spools nailed on might make a fine tractor. The dried mowed grass is good for pretend hay.

Picture in your mind a front porch with a pair of rockers occupied by two elderly gentlemen discussing world affairs. The more intense the discussion, the faster those chairs are rocking. Not a good place for a cat.

A front porch would be a nice place for an afternoon tea. Ladies with their knitting or crewel embroidery discussing the last Ladies Aid meeting, or who would be the next president of their group. They probably also are discussing a new recipe somewhere in the conversation.

The front porch would be a nice place to relax after a hard days work and just watch the cars go by.

A porch swing could probably tell stories of young lovers spending long hours into the night, day dreaming of a long and happy life together.

Porches are beneficial 24 hours a day. My front porch isn't big enough for a rocker and the back isn't suited to a deck so the rocking chair will have to stay in the dining room.

Do you suppose front porches have been replaced by the backyard deck—patio? Backyard patios are inviting with umbrella picnic tables, matching chairs, and a barbecue grill going with the succulent aroma of steak wafting through the neighborhood. I wonder how long it will be until someone decides charcoal smoke is pollution?

Radio is Still Important in our Lives even with Television, Tapes, and CDs.

I remember when I was about in the 5th grade in school reading a Weekly Reader—that years down the road people would be watching movies in the comfort of their homes. Unthinkable! Could this possibly be true—that you could watch a show in your home? Going to the show only cost 10 cents; however, 10 cents was hard to come by, so the movie theatre was a special occasion. A birthday or a Shirley Temple movie would be acceptable reasons to go.

Radio was the main means of communication and entertainment. Radios at that time had tubes and every so often a tube would have to be replaced in order for it to work. Sometimes a good whack would jar it enough to finish a good story.

Can't you remember sitting up close to the radio with your ear in the speaker so you didn't miss a word or a soapy or the news?

Radio stations were few, so WDAY was the main station with lots of entertainment. Mornings included "The Breakfast Club" and "The Kitchen Club" with Edit Hanson. With a Perfex box top you could order recipes. Noontime featured Ken Kennedy with news and various entertainment. Pat Kelly was organist; Linda Lou was a singer. Hank and Thelma san and yodeled songs like "Horsy keep your tail up," "Keep the sun out of my eyes," etc. There was "Lem Hawkins," The Fairmount Old Timers, Ole Swenson and his singing violin, Cedric and Adams singing and guitar, Frank Scott-pianist, Red Royer band from Wahpeton: Red Royer, trumpet; Jim McCullough, drums; Mary Ann Meyer, piano; and John Stall, tenor sax. Sunday morning was religious with O. E. MC Cracken with the Fargo Union Mission. Sunday afternoon and evening included "The Shadow," "The Green Hornet," and "Jack Benny." Weekday matinees were the soapies,

whereby a certain degree of quiet was insisted on so Mom didn't miss a word of "Ma Perkins," "One Man's Family," "Judy and Jane," and "Stella Dellas." During the week evenings included "The Great Gildersleeve," "Fibber McGee and Molly," "Little Orphan Annie," and "Dick Tracy." H. B. Kultenborn was the National News Commentator. Saturday mornings were geared to the children. Some of the favorites were "Roy Rogers and Trigger," "The Lone Ranger and Tonto," "The Little Rascals," and "Smilin' Ed and Froggy." These were good entertainment and kept squabbles to a minimum.

It was about the late 50s when transistor radios came into being; thus you could carry radios in your pocket or go jogging with headphones.

With radio, you pictured the scenes in your mind and imagine what was going on. With TV, everything is presented in picture, thus no brain strain.

It's time for my soapy, so I will put the TV on and not strain my brain by watching the events while I have my coffee.

Gee! Has the Weekly Reader been around that long?!

Give up Today's Appliances? No Way!

*I*f you had a choice, which of your appliances would you give up? How about your range? There are so many ways to prepare food without the range. If there are a few small appliances in a person's kitchen, they could get by.

In the early part of the century, there were no refrigerators so improvisation was needed to keep foods cool. Now the refrigerator is a necessity.

Then let's consider the clothes dryer. I could manage quite well without one. However, if I had a family at home I'm sure I'd think twice about giving it up.

When I think back to the day before electric and gas clothes dryers, women used ropes or wire that hung from post to post in the backyard. In the middle of the winter, they used a nail pounded into each doorframe with lines strung from door to door to hasten the drying process.

The white clothes had to be hung outside to freeze. It proved to be a struggle to get the clothes in the door. Oh yes, it proved plenty of moisture in the house but also provided unexplained colds and sore throats.

When the children were in the diaper stage it seemed that diapers, having to be washed frequently, became part of the winter decor. I remember when my youngest brother was born. I was in high school and after school would have to go straight home to wash diapers and hang them on a clothes rack to dry. I vowed to myself that some day Larry would chop wood for me. Larry never did chop wood for me, mainly because I was not in need of it. He gave me a lot of joy in other ways, though.

By the time I got a clothes dryer, my brood was long past the diaper stage. In the days of diapers it seemed tots were trained as soon as possible in order to be rid of the "daily diaper-washing chore." A dryer isn't really necessary for diapers today with the availability of the "disposable diaper." However, if I were a *working outside the home Mom,* the dryer would be a keeper.

I do enjoy hanging clothes outside, weather permitting, so my dryer is mainly a winter convenience.

Clotheslines are noted as being "for the birds." They sit either on them or under them, so care must be taken when hanging out or bringing in clothes so a person doesn't drop them.

As long as I can, I will hang clothes out to dry in the summer. I don't have to be concerned about the birds under the lines, though—just the ones that fly over.

Resolutions Don't Have to be Such a Bad Thing

*N*ow that we have the Christmas season over, I'm wondering how many people have spent time between Christmas and New Years making resolutions.

Here's my list:

1. Go on a diet—have some fudge.
2. Exercise more—forget it.
3. Do dishes after each meal—wait until the sink is full.
4. Take a daily bath—do only as time permits or necessary.
5. Take the garbage out every day—every other day.

6. Save money to put in savings—only if there isn't too much month at the end of the money.

7. Cut down on mall hopping—take in all the after-Christmas sales.

8. Cut down on the hour-long phone calls—at least wait 15 minutes between in case someone else is trying to call.

9. Practice writing "98" so you aren't writing "97" until July.

10. Get to work on time—go late. It will probably make a statement, probably from a VIP.

Wasn't that easy to make all those resolutions and so much fun to break without feeling guilty?

I think everyone would agree that the first resolution is probably on everyone's "No. 1 to do list." Is everyone using their new Christmas treadmill, stationary bike or weight lifting machine? I don't have a treadmill or weights, but I do have a nearly new stationary bike. I mean it is stationary.

After the holidays I'm going to get started peddling. My intention is five miles a day. Gee, that sounds like a lot for just starting. I should start out easy—say two miles a day.

The bicycle is noisy so watching TV isn't the best to make the miles add up. Maybe an informative book, thus improving the mind and circulation.

A good excuse for not exercising now is the weather is lovely and I can still get out and do things. But if we get a lot of snow and I am housebound, then will be a good time to start.

I have found a lot of reasons why not to exercise. They easily outweigh the reasons I should. Oh what the heck! Let's have a cup of coffee and maybe we can find a piece or two of leftover Christmas fudge.

Buying for Valentine's Day was a Big Decision for a Child to Make

*V*alentine's Day is a very important one. Thinking back to my school days, it almost ranked up there with Christmas.

Valentines came in assorted styles back then, just as they do now. They were anywhere from two for a penny on up. The better valentines might even have a stick of gum or a sucker. Oh what a treat, especially if treats were a rarity at home.

My sister and I would each be given a nickel. We could either buy five valentines for a penny each or get 10 valentines for 5 cents if we bought the two for a penny. When you are eight years old, that is a major decision since there were so many cards to choose from.

Thinking back, there might be a very special one that would be for your dearest friend, which at that age would no doubt be a girl. But now came the bigger decision. Who to get the 10 valentines to when there were 25 in the class?

Sure we could pick out 10 favorite classmates and put their name on. Wait a minute. I liked Betty too. Now I had to erase Mary's name and put Betty's name at the top. But Mary wouldn't talk to me if I didn't give her one and she always gave me one, so I had to erase Betty to put Mary on again.

When the day finally arrived for handing out the valentines, it was such fun to be the one chosen to pass them out.

I remember taking my package of valentines home and reading and re-reading them until they showed signs of wearing out. They'd eventually be discarded.

How did Valentine's Day come about anyway? Valentines were first made in the early 1800s. St. Valentine is the patron saint of lovers—a day which lovers traditionally exchange affectionate messages. Valentines can be sweet, humorous or very ornate with dried flowers, feathers, imitation jewels, mother of pearl or seashells.

Another tradition is to send your sweetheart candy or flowers.

I'm wondering whether my mailbox will hold all my valentines this year. Maybe I need to put up a special one.

Using Every Color in the Rainbow makes a "Pretty" Easter Egg

*S*o there's nothing on the menu for supper. What to do? I go the refrigerator and pull out an egg or two. There are so many things to do with eggs besides baking. Eggs can be scrambled, soft boiled, hard-boiled, fried, made into an omelet and so much more.

I feel next to Christmas or birthdays, children enjoy Easter as one of their favorite holidays. Where else can they paint pretty Easter eggs with pastel and oil colors?

There are just as many ways of buying eggs as there are preparing them. There are jelly bean eggs, malted milk eggs, decorated eggs with creamy nugget filling, marshmallow with chocolate covering, marshmallow with sweet-colored sugar, just to name a few.

The plastic-coated eggs are pretty on a tree branch and are extra special when filled with candy.

Perhaps the favorite way of using an egg at Easter time is coloring them.

As far as I can find, years ago the only coloring agent was putting yellow onionskins in the water as the eggs were cooking.

Now there are endless ways of decorating eggs, such as a package of the basic pastels with the wax pencil to write names of a friend or your own, without forgetting Grandma and Grandpa of course.

The oil paints make a pretty egg, making it look marbleized when lifted out of the water.

I have seen pictures of eggs decorated Ukrainian-style. They are so lovely and delicate, appearing almost reverent with their colors. To own one would almost make a person feel like royalty.

My favorite is the Cadbury egg. I'll put that on my list of Easter goodies.

When my children colored eggs, they would sometimes use each color for one egg. The end result was a hideous color concoction. To me they were beautiful, especially if my name was on it.

I liked decorating eggs by first blowing out the middle and then placing a colorful plastic sleeve over it. To do this, dip the egg in warm water and the plastic shrinks to fit the egg. They keep for years with careful handling. Another alternative would be crocheting a cover.

I don't think there was ever an answer as to which came first, the chicken or the egg. Thinking about it, though, eggs are usually found in a nest. How did they get there?

Eggs are quite versatile, a great creation. Often there are recipes that call for brine or curing meat or for pickles with the brine having to be strong enough to float an egg.

Years ago, eggs were preserved for the winter season when hens went on strike. The eggs were kept in salt brine.

Thinking back to the days of my children coloring eggs and being so proud of their artwork was worth reflecting on and a memory I treasure.

Kisses Went to Bearers of Colorful May Baskets

"May Day!" "May Day!"

No, this isn't an SOS signal. Remember way back to that May 1st art class in school when we made May baskets? They were made of construction paper for those of you who don't remember the projects.

We chose from our favorite colors and were given a pattern to trace. I remember carefully cutting the basket out and pasting it together. By the time I had the last corner pasted, the first one was loose. Paste just wasn't the quality we have today. Then I finally had to hold the glued spot until it was dry before going on to the next corner. Children who were very artistic, cut out some flowers and leaves for added beauty.

The walk home was fraught with peril. We walked fast and prayed our basket wouldn't fall apart before you got there.

Once home, Easter grass could have been put in the bottom layered with candy. We delivered it to our best friend's house and hung it on the doorknob, then ran away and hid.

It was hung outright so they'd find it right away, then were able to run out and catch the deliverer to kiss them. By the time we got home we might have one on our doorknob.

In many countries, May Day is celebrated as a spring festival. It marks the arrival of life in early spring after winter. Children often gather flowers to place in homemade paper May baskets to hand on the doorknobs of friends and neighbors on May Day morning. May is also a time for courting. The celebrations date back to medieval times.

The old Farmers Almanac tells us that May baskets were hung on the door to welcome spring. It is stated that dew collected on May Day is reputed to wash away freckles.

May basket floral bouquets were once more articulate than the fountain pen. Some significant flowers included apple blossoms for temptation, buttercups for childishness and riches, chamomile for energy in adversity, white daisies for innocence, purple lilacs for modesty, mountain ash for prudence, yellow tulips for hopeless love, sweet peas for respect and blue violets for faithfulness.

Wouldn't May Day celebrations be most acceptable practices in this day? Even lovely dandelions in a homemade May basket would brighten any Mom or Grandma's day. They might even offer a cup of hot cocoa or lemonade.

Although, it could be disappointing if your very best friend didn't find your basket while you waited.

Mouth-Watering Ice Cream Perfect for 4th

*I*s there anything better than the taste of ice cream? I remember as a child relishing an ice cream cone to the last bite. Would you believe an ice cream cone was 5 cents? A triple-decker was 10 cents, and a pint of ice cream was 15 cents. Divide that among four people. Every spoonful was savored.

A 10-cent triple-decker cone was very rare, mostly unaffordable.

Ice cream was mostly a summertime treat. Later in life I was quite amazed to find out that ice cream could be made in the winter as well. The necessities would be the crank ice cream freezer and a willing person to go to the creek or wherever for ice. You needed lots of salt, cream, eggs and a person to crank the freezer, sometimes a two-person job. It was a long chore so by the end of the freezing time you may have needed a relief person.

When the freezing was complete, being first in line with a big spoon to clean the beater and get the first lick was almost reason enough to push and shove if more siblings waited in line. Then the cover was replaced on the can so it could set a while.

In the meantime, you cooked the chocolate topping and got the soda crackers out. Soda crackers? They say it was very good. However, I could never even try salty soda crackers with delicious ice cream.

Everybody has their own favorite recipe for homemade ice cream. Some just put everything in the can and cranked it, while others preferred cooked custard prepared early so it would cool. You could also have added you favorite flavors and nuts.

I don't imaging a nutritionist would have though much of this, but homemade ice cream was our Sunday evening supper. Of course Sunday noon meal was ample and provided nutrients sufficient for the day.

Living on the farm provided the necessities for ice cream—eggs, milk and cream which when poured was thick and rich. In the winter, ice was plentiful.

As I scanned my 1936 Watkins Cookbook, I saw so many variations. Ginger glace ice cream, French chocolate ice cream, strawberry ice cream, maple parfait, orange sherbet...I found in the later recipe books only the variations for vanilla, basically the same, however, all mouth-watering, tempting and leaving me wishing a person could chase out the calories.

Very seldom were there leftovers.

Today, you can buy ice cream by the plastic pail, a half-gallon, cone, sundae, whatever. But nothing beats the tin can.

Remember when you are making you July 4th homemade ice cream with the electric freezer to be sure to use salt—not sugar for freezing.

Jim, let's get out the freezer and show the boys and Monticello, Minn., city slickers what real ice cream is for the 4th.

Just a reminder, don't forget to fly your flag.

Thank Heaven for Handiwipes

Cars and people have been bombarded the past few years with bumper stickers, banners and mugs with mottos or special endearments.

Many people have something in their possession that might say "No. 1 Dad," "No. 1 Nurse," "Nurses give TLC," or something to that effect.

There are special cups for almost any personality or occasion. Several years ago my daughter presented me with a mug with the inscription, "Mom, I'll always love you but I'll never forgive you for washing my face with spit on a hankie!"

Guilty as charged.

But at the time, I guess it was the thing to do Sunday mornings when you were readying four children for church. By the time the last child was clean and you were ready, and then had the last one in the car, there wasn't any time for a face check until you were cruising down the road.

With three youngsters in the backseat and one on my lap, some sense told me to turn around to make a face check. I wasn't too surprised to see a milk mustache, a chocolate milk beard or grape jelly from ear-to-ear.

What to do?

Fumble in my purse or pocket to hopefully find a hankie, a clean one, so I could stick it on my tongue and go from one to the other until everything was erased—hopefully.

I don't think there are too many parents who haven't gone through some kind of ordeal like this. No, I actually didn't spit on my hankie, just moistened it on my tongue.

As I'm sipping on a mug of whatever, I'm thinking, "thank heaven for today's handiwipes."

CHRISTMAS

A Modern Christmas Story

*T*he Bible tells us that Jesus was born in a stable. Let's put Jesus' birth in a modern day setting.

Mary is scurrying around her modest home and announces to Joseph that her time has come and he should get the car warmed for their trip to the hospital. It is quite a way to the hospital so we should hurry. There are several stoplights on the way and most of them could be red! As we are on our way we encounter a detour: St. Andrews Hospital detour—8 blocks west, 5 blocks north, and 10 blocks east. It is cold outside and the roads are slick in spots. In good time we arrive at a large, brightly lit building. Joseph assists Mary from the car and they enter the lobby with a thick carpet on the floor, colorful plush furniture and lovely green plants in various bright places. The atmosphere is very pleasant and Mary is more at ease. Joseph approaches the desk and gives the receptionist the necessary information. Joseph and Mary are told to "have a seat," somebody would be there to escort them to the Maternity Ward. In a short time, a nurse in a white uniform and a perky little hat is pushing a wheel chair for Mary to ride in. They get on an elevator and ride several floors to the Maternity Ward where Mary is ushered into a pleasant room. The walls are basic white with curtains and a bedspread in colors to match the carpet.

After the babe is born, he is in a bassinet and there is something special about this baby. The Holy Spirit has told the nurses that this baby is a special gift to the world. He will save us from our sins.

He weighted in at 7 lbs. 12 oz. and is 19 inches long. He has very little hair and is very content. The nurses realize that this baby is special, call the newspapers and TV stations that Mary has given birth to a baby boy that is so special he will save us from our sins. In the morning we turn on our TV and see a "Special News Announcement." "News of a Savior has been received by our news office. Watch the 6 o'clock news for the latest news on this event." The TV reporters and newspaper reporters are hurrying to the hospital to be the first to see this marvel. On their arrival, they look in awe through a big glass window—and notice a halo around his head. They anxiously await his first cry or just a wiggle of a finger for their camera crew. In the meantime, reporters are interviewing Joseph and Mary with detailed questions about the birth. After they leave, Mary is tired and wants to sleep.

The news stations are hurriedly getting their stories prepared for the 6 o'clock news. The announcement might go like this:

Earlier today our station received a call stating that a healthy baby boy has been born at St. Andrews Hospital to Joseph and Mary of Nazareth. It is said He will save us from our sins. No name has been chosen at this time. Stay tuned for more information at a later time.

A young musician who has tried many times to hit the top ten on the music chart has picked up on the announcement and has an idea for a song. How about the title "Beebop beebop the baby Jesus is born, yah, yah, yah!"? Sure to get a gold record.

Joseph and Mary took their baby home to watch him grow in wisdom and gladden their hearts. I don't think Joseph handed out cigars. Mary is given a box of complimentary gifts from different companies advertising their products, which include a bottle of milk, baby oils and powders, and several boxes of disposable diapers.

Imagine the surprised looks on the nurses faces when they realize what an unusual child has been placed in their care.

The Night Before Christmas

"*T*he Night Before Christmas" is one of the Christmas poems I have been able to remember and enjoy. Let's read the poem:

The Night Before Christmas

By Samuel Clemens Moore

Twas the night before Christmas
When all through the house
Not a creature was stirring
Not even a mouse.

The stockings were hung by the chimney with care
In hopes that St. Nicholas soon would be there.
The children were nestled all snug in their beds
While visions of sugarplums danced in their heads.

Mama in her kerchief and I in my cap
Had just settled down for a long winter's nap.
When out on the lawn there arose such a clatter
I sprang from my bed to see what was the matter.

Away to the window I flew like a flash,
Tore open the shutters and threw up the sash.
The moon on the breast of the new fallen snow,

Gave a luster to midday to objects below.

When what to my wondering eyes should appear?
But a miniature sleight and eight tiny reindeer;
With a little old driver so lively and quick,
I knew in a moment in must be St. Nick.

More rapid than eagles his coursers they came,
And he whistled and shouted and called them by name:
"Now, Dasher! Now, Dancer! Now, Prancer and Vixen!
On, Comet! On Cupid! On Donner and Blitzen!
To the top of the porch, to the top of the wall!
Now dash away, dash away, dash away all.'
As dry leaves that before the wild hurricane fly,
When they meet with an obstacle, mount to the sky.

So up to the housetop the coursers they flew,
With a sleigh full of toys and St. Nicholas too.
And then in a twinkling I heard on the roof,
The prancing and pawing of each little hoof.

As I drew in my head and was turning around
Down the chimney St. Nicholas came with a bound.
He was dressed all in fur from his head to his foot,
His clothes were all tarnished with ashes and soot.

A bundle of toys he had flung on his back
And he looked like a peddler just opening his pack.
His eyes how they twinkled! His dimples how merry!
His cheeks were like roses, his nose like a cherry.

His droll little mouth was drawn up like a bow,

And the beard on his chin was a white as the snow.
The stump of a pipe he held tight in his teeth,
And the smoke, it encircled his head like a wreath.

He had a broad face and a little round belly
That shook when he laughed like a bowl full of jelly.
He was chubby and plump, a right jolly old elf,
And I laughed when I saw him in spite of myself.

A wink of his eye and a twist of his head,
Soon gave me to know I had nothing to dread.
He spoke not a word but went straight to his work
And filled all the stockings, then turned with a jerk,

And laying a finger aside of his nose,
Giving a nod up the chimney he rose.
He sprang to his sleigh, to his team gave a whistle,
And away they all flew like the down of a thistle.
But I heard him exclaim as he drove out of sight,
"Merry Christmas to all, and to all a good night!

Let's take a look at this poem today. Yes, the children are snug in their beds, but visions of sugarplums? They would think more in terms of computer games, CD players, and electronic paraphernalia.

Can't you just see mama in her kerchief? There's papa in his nightshirt and cap, dashing to the window to whip open the shutters and throw open the sash.

Can't you remember lying awake every Christmas Eve waiting for the aforementioned spectacle when you were a child? You listened so hard for the prancing and pawing of hooves on the roof. You tried so hard to stay awake to outsmart Santa so you could get just a glimpse of him. Then you'd awaken and find out you had gone to sleep and missed it all.

Even in this day of electronics, I don't think you could improve on the ditty of Santa laying his finger aside of his nose and ascending the chimney. Do you suppose Santa has an electronic computer panel on his sleigh, which is wired to the lead reindeer through the reins? This would certainly simplify the workload and speed up the trip. I think it would be a good idea to put the makings for hot chocolate out for Santa. He could warm it in the microwave while he places his treats around the tree.

While my grandson Adam and I were having coffee and "tookies" one day, I read the poem to him. He was quite intrigued by it and wanted to hear it again. No matter what age, next to the story of the birth of Jesus, this story will remain high in the favorite category for young and old alike.

So deck the halls and celebrate the holidays with cheer.

Bells

*P*eople who collect things are very interesting to visit with. Collectors take great pride in their hobby. They put a lot of TLC into it besides the monetary value. Some of the things included in a collectors hobby would include dolls, postage stamps, coins, tea cups and saucers, salt and pepper shaker sets, dishes, kerosene lamps, and horses, just to name a few. I have a miniature bell collection, and I try to collect money, but for some reason there always seems to be too much month at the end of the money. Now that the Christmas season is approaching I thought it would be interesting to find out how and where bells originated. Bells are synonymous with Christmas as well as having had many purposes over the years. Remember the cowbell? The bell on the country school, the bell on the teacher's desk if order was needed. Bells to commemorate anniversaries, wedding bells, church bells, clarions, bells ring to call order, and bells might announce mealtime. Patients in hospitals used to have a bell to ring for attention. Babies have bells on their shoelaces. Jesters had bells on their hats. The telephone bell, which has been replaced with a not-so-pleasant buzzer. Bells were used in the Victorian era to summon the maid or butler. Songs have been written about bells, as well as poetry. Bells are used for many kinds of decorations. A child's toy that has bells is sure to bring out a smile. Doorbells announce visitors. Just think of a sleigh being pulled by a beautiful team of horses and the harness is adorned with bells that jingle as the team trots along with a sleigh full of happy, laughing riders as they sing, "Over the River and Through the Woods." Bells have a pleasant sound that is pleasing to the audio part of the anatomy; besides, there is something cheerful about a bell. Doesn't a bell choir have the most calming, delightful sound peeling out "Silent Night?"

While I'm sipping my afternoon coffee, I'm wondering how the word "bell" originated and after visiting our local library and doing a little research in the Britannica Encyclopedia, I discovered the bell is derived from Anglo-Saxon "bellam" meaning to "bellow." Stoves, dishes, pots of hammered metal and cast bronze all have a certain ring and it may be that the more or less resonant tone of such vessels was known and utilized as a form of amusement and signal. Bells date back to 500 A.D. at the beginning of the Bronze Age. A cup used as the general form, developed the technique of ringing bells by means of a clapper striking from inside. The first bells were made from a flat plate with the corners cut out, then beat and riveted in a square or oblong shape. These bells were brought to Ireland by St. Patrick and Palladius the first missionaries from Rome about 450 A.D. I didn't realize bells dated back that far. While you are thinking about a Christmas gift for someone, how about a nice group of battery operated bells that start ringing when you walk up to the door.

Bells are even electro-mechanical but I would rather do it myself. We can't forget the Liberty Bell, our symbol of freedom, or the bells that call us to church on Sunday morning and Christmas.

Christmas Trees 25¢ or 10¢

I have been trying to remember as far back as I can to the Christmas I remember first. All I can come up with is at the age of 5; I got a coloring book and colors for Christmas. I enjoyed the coloring book so much. It seemed that every picture I colored was one less to enjoy later on.

I am remembering about the time I was 10 years old, an aunt and uncle lived at Baudette, Minnesota, and they raised Christmas trees, the short-needled kind. They must have found a good outlet in the Wahpeton area. Every December, they would bring a truckload to Wahpeton. They were our guests until the trees were sold.

Uncle Jay would let me sell the trees to the neighbors at 25 cents for a tall tree and 10 cents for a short tree. My profit was 1 cent.

After selling my first tree, I had a humongous decision to make. The decision that it would go to the candy store for a 2-for-a-penny candy was no problem at all. The big decision was what kind. I liked "guess what's" which was two candy kisses with a surprise, licorice cigars, the hard black kind, snaps or marshmallow stars. It was the marshmallow stars. I would take just one small bite a day to ration this tasty morsel as long as possible, until the marshmallow was getting dry and sticky. Boy, it really stretched!

Christmas trees today come in so many varieties—long and short-needles, colored, and flocked. Needless-to-say, they are beautiful, but for 10 cents or 25 cents? I don't think so. The 10 and 25 centers were 55 years ago. But with some strung popcorn and cranberries, and a few glittering balls, candy canes and lights, with a beautiful star or angel on top, it would make even a sorry tree into a thing of beauty.

Purchasing a tree today can be a family outing, with each member of the family picking one that they think would fit into the family home, envisioning it all decorated. Each one would think their choice was the best. How do we decide to everyone's pleasure? We'll take time out for a cup of hot cider or hot chocolate and then make our decision.

Each Child Must Learn
Their Carols, Recitations

*I*t has been a common practice for many years where the Sunday School students have a Christmas program. I believe this goes way back to beyond my own childhood.

I remember the preparation that had to be done in the short Advent season. Christmas carols were learned and each child was given a piece commensurate to their age. Parents worked with their children to make sure each knew their recitations to be recited verbatim so they wouldn't embarrass anyone.

Then the props were gathered for the program and improvements made where necessary.

Just as in the past, church most always has a beautiful Christmas tree, purchased or donated, but always decorated by the senior members. The peak is adorned with an angel or a star. Lots of lights and garland and colorful balls add to the beauty of the Christmas tree for the Christ child. The front doors and windows are adorned with wreaths with a big red bow and boughs of evergreen on the ledges.

Outside will be the creche or the manger scene. Mary and Joseph are looking down on the Baby Jesus in his humble crib, wrapped in swaddlings.

Let's go back to the day of the program. Oh yes, the new dresses have to be fit properly with shirt and pants neatly pressed. Curls have to be prepared early and ribbons tied on to match the dresses.

Now that the day of the program has finally arrived, we are all ready and know (hopefully) our recitations, otherwise threats have been made that Santa Claus won't bring the doll I've been wanting or the train that chugs around on its track.

The class marches into the front of the church with our parents and grandparents anxiously awaiting our recitations. After all the horsing around at practice the teachers are wondering whether there is any way possible this could be a success. But everyone earnestly does their part. It doesn't really matter if there's a word or two missed here, or a line reversed there.

After the program is over, treats are passed out and we children are anxious to start opening our bags and are admonished to wait until we get home.

But wait—we aren't finished. The organist starts to play "Silent Night" and everyone is quiet and joins in.

Silent night
Holy night
All is calm,
All is bright,
Round yon Virgin Mother and Child
Holy infant so tender and mild
Sleep in heavenly peace
Sleep in heavenly peace

This carol has a calming effect. As we leave for home, there is a good possibility that Santa Claus has been there. He always comes to our house while we're at Christmas Eve services. When we were in the car and ready to go, for some strange reason Dad always seems to forget a hankie or his billfold and he has to make a last-second trip into the house. No matter.

We can ponder that while we have a cup of coffee and think about getting Christmas cards ready to mail. It's always a pleasure to wish kith and kin a "Merry Christmas" and most always takes more than one cup of coffee.

Merry Christmas everyone!

Christmas Carols

*T*his time of year, no matter where you go, Christmas carols are wafting through malls, in the stores, and even streets. Christmas carols bring the spirit out in young and old.

Caroling began in Medieval England. The word "carol" is thought to be derived from the medieval French word that means a round dance.

Christmas carols can be merry, solemn, or impressive, like Handel's "Messiah" or Pavarotti singing "Adeste Fidelis." Merry carols might be "Jingle Bells," "O Tannenbaum," or Tschaikovsky's "Nutcracker" ballet. There's nothing so solemn as listening to a children's choir singing "Silent Night" or visiting a retirement home and hearing "Stille Naught" sung by the residents.

Is there anything more heart-warming than Christmas carolers coming to your home with sounds of familiar songs echoing through the house? I've had second thoughts about relating this episode, but I guess I will. Last year one Sunday evening before Christmas, there was a knock on my door. I went to the door and found my grandson Aaron and his friend Anthony. Nothing unusual about that. Expecting to be asked for a favor, I went to the window and shook my head "no" and stuck my tongue out at them.

Aaron knows Grandma will let him in regardless. I opened the door and in came 20 carolers. I was so embarrassed. One of my many most embarrassing moments.

There should be a moral to this story, which I will heed from now on. The carolers filled my kitchen and entry and sang the carols. They were an important part of Christmas for me, probably as important to he people who hear carolers visiting retirement homes and shut ins.

The classic Christmas carol "Silent Night" was written by Franz Gruber in 1818. On Christmas Eve that year the church organ broke down in the Church of St. Nicolas, Odendorf, Austria. This was a catastrophe for all the music was arranged with organ accompaniment in mind. The assistant pastor, Joseph Mohr, handed the organist Franz Gruber a carol he had written suggesting that he arrange it for guitar and two solo voices thus saving the day for a musical celebration. The song was sung that night, but might have been forgotten but for the organ builder who came to repair the organ after Christmas and heard the carol. He was so impressed with "Silent Night" or "Stile Naught" that he took a copy with him on his rounds through the region thus beginning its popularity.

While you have your second cup of coffee, put on a Christmas tape or CD and sing along. Merry Christmas everyone.

Over the Back Fence

Be Careful What You Eat with Your Coffee

I must relate an incident that happened at my house. You could call it humorous, or something else.

Recently, my grandson Aaron spent the night here. In the morning after he left for school I noticed a plastic bag on the floor by the back door. I was picking up garbage, since it was garbage day. I was going to drop it in the garbage. But, my better judgment told me to check it out. Next week I could be looking for something and it would be exactly what I garbaged. So, I opened the plastic bag to find four smaller plastic bags with a neat square in them.

I thought Laurie sent me bars. Isn't that nice of her? I closed the bag thinking, "I'll have a bar with my coffee later on." But on the way to the refrigerator, curiosity got the best of me. I had to see what kind of bars they were so I took out a bag and looked.

Chocolate?

It hit me like a ton of bricks. I got a whiff of cow manure. It was Aaron's science fair project. Needless-to-say, it was put back in its original place.

Aaron, maybe next year you could try kite flying or something that Grandma won't have with her coffee.

The moral of this story is, "be careful what you have with your coffee." It could be a science fair project.

Swing Along

*M*y house is rather small. Since there isn't a lot of room for exercise, during the winter, I frequently stroll to the kitchen window to see what the temperature is. My granddaughter, Karen and her husband Larry, fixed a large thermometer to the frame of my lawn swing so I could easily see the temperature from the kitchen window.

Being somewhat housebound in the winter, this fete can become the excitement for the day. While I was writing this column, I looked at the thermometer. It was 0 degrees. I also looked at the swing and saw only the top 6 inches of the back, while the rest was buried under a foot of snow.

As we contemplate spring, let's look at what a swing can do for our morale. To a child it is a challenge. To people like me, who need a break in their day, it is a very relaxing way to come back to reality.

As a child, there was a poem I was fond of that went like this: *"How would you like to go up in a swing? Up in the sky so high."*

Everyone, young and old, should have a swing. When we were children we spent many hours on a swing. Learning to pump our legs was a real challenge. One had to work at the fete to accomplish it. But once done, it provided hours of entertainment.

Swings come in models for all ages and sizes. Babies have their own style to provide them safety. Some are even automated so Mom is free to do other things while the baby is being entertained.

When we were a little older, we had swings made out of a gunnysack stuffed sufficiently with straw and tied securely to a tall tree branch with a rope. I remember taking a swift run and then jumping on the sack. We'd hang on and see who could ride the longest. There was another type of swing fashioned out of a car tire, securely tied to a rope. On this, you could go round and round, it might cause some dizziness, but it was oh so much fun!

Then we had the board swing hung by ropes or a chain. Oh, you could go so high, soaring through the air with your hair flying loose in the air. When the swing slowed down, you might be real brave and could jump off to see how far you could get before landing.

The wintertime doesn't interfere with swinging if you are fortunate enough to have a barn packed with hay. What a thrill it is to soar through the air and land in a pile of soft hay. Of course, your elders shouldn't be aware of such goings on.

A lovely accompaniment to a backyard is to see a swing or the more modern swing sets that also have other exercise equipment. Whenever swings are noted in a backyard, you can be sure there are sounds of children echoing through the neighborhood with shouts of "my turn." How abut the thrill of hearing a child yelling, "Look at me, mom," while their mother's heart is thumping away and she's saying a silent prayer.

Sometimes after a rain, there was a mud puddle beneath the swing. We couldn't possibly go around it, so the mud showed up on our mother's kitchen floor.

Some might say I'm in my second childhood because I have a swing in my back yard. It was a gift from my daughter who was moving too far to take it along. I was overjoyed at the thought of having a swing. Needless-to-say, I lost no time in recruiting two sons to move it for me. This swing has given numerous hours of joy and entertainment to neighbors, friends and family. My neighbor will stick her head in the door and say, "It's so nice, let's swing awhile." Being in full agreement, and needing no further persuasion, I take my hands out of the dishwater and join her on the swing with a cup of coffee.

Swinging is enjoyable any time of the day. In the morning, I rest on the swing after gardening or working in the flower garden. In the afternoon, it's perfect with a refreshing drink for a break from mowing the lawn, or even just relaxing in the evening. You know I've even had a few talks with the Lord out there.

Here I am looking out my window at 6 inches of snow and a 9-degree day. I am hoping spring will come soon so I can call over to my neighbor and say, "Come and swing awhile."

One more trip to the window and the temperature has gone up a few degrees. I won't be having my second cup of coffee out on the swing today. It will be taken at the dining room table as I surf the TV channels and long for spring. I was thinking the sooner spring comes, the sooner winter will be here again.

When the snow goes away, come and sit on my swing and reminisce with me.

Teachers

*S*chool is again in full swing. It always brings me back to my old school days.

I am sure most of us had a favorite teacher in their past, or even the present. A teacher we remember for being kind. Perhaps they were a strict disciplinarian. We may have admired our teacher for other reasons—because they set good examples and you thought you wanted to be that kind of person when you grew up.

I recall a teacher from years past. She was a substitute teacher. When I saw Mrs. Rothwell was teaching I knew I would learn for sure that day. When she walked into the room and stood by her desk there was instant quiet and respect. She didn't have to say a word. One look around the room was sufficient.

She had a way of presenting her lessons that made learning easy for every student. She had a way of holding our attention and keeping it, leaving little time for idle thought, trickery or mischief. She was a very pleasant person.

Another teacher I remember is Mr. Jenson. He still lives in Breckenridge, Minnesota. He taught 10th grade biology. He was a very good teacher, but I didn't like biology. I absorbed only enough to pass, or he passed me out of the goodness of his heart. My apologies to Mr. Jenson. I realize now he was doing his job. I wasn't. He still has some hair even today.

I remember two Sunday school teachers among the many I had. There was Mrs. Augustine from Wahpeton. I was about 8 years old when I was in her class. She was such a caring person. She had given each of us a picture for Christmas. I still have mine. I had written on the back of it, "1938."

Then there was Sarah Clark from Breckenridge, a very jolly, Christian lady. She loved everybody. I had visited with her in later years, and she was still a loving person.

As I reflect over my second cup of coffee, I'm wondering how many of my teachers would like to tell me, "I told you so…" or "This is how life would be…", or "This is why you are learning."

Thanks for everything.

Ethnic Holidays

The Germans have Oktober Fest, the Irish have St. Patrick's Day and Norwegians have Syttende Mai. So far I think that means Seventeenth of May, but I may have to do some research as to why.

The Germans celebrate their heritage with the Oktober Fest and their "Oompa bands," Polka dances and bar maids that can carry seven beer steins without batting an eyelash. You really don't see a lot of advertising of Oktober Fest promotions in the stores. I assume there is a lot of elbow bending and some skull cramps after a few days of celebrating.

The Irish celebrate St. Patrick's Day with a lot of decorum. You see lots of advertising with Shamrocks, Gremlins, banners, green beer, corned beef and cabbage meals that are a delicacy for me and a must eat on St. Patty's Day. The three Irish Tenors have become quite popular with their Irish folk songs. There are lots of Pat and Mike jokes—some acceptable and some not so acceptable, but you can find humor in both. The larger cities have St. Patrick's Day parades.

There aren't a lot of decorations for Syttende Mai in this area. No advertising or national flower or memorable figures. I would guess the Norwegians would start the day with a Norwegian Bubble Bath, then a break fast of Norwegian donuts. Lunch would probably be Lutefisk and Lefse. I have never eaten Lutefisk, which is to a Norwegian what corned beef and cabbage are to an Irishman. I have heard pros and cons about it, however, I can't fathom anything being edible that has to be soaked in lye before it can be eaten or even have food value after being soaked in lye. I have seen several recipes for Norwegian pastries for which they are noted. I can't forget Ole and Lena jokes, which are comparable to Pat and Mike jokes.

I think that with my coffee I'll have some Danish rolls or a Norwegian donut hole. I did my homework and found out that Syttende Mai is Norwegian Independence Day. Happy Norwegian Independence Day to all Norwegians and Norwegian wanna bees.

Hours of Fun could be Had with Paper Dolls

Remember back to when you were a child, when a favorite birthday gift was coloring and paper doll books. One could be purchased for 10 cents.

Paper doll books were fashioned after popular movie stars. The Dionne quintuplets were very popular in the 30s, as were Sonja Henie and Shirley Temple to name a few.

In the summer, I remember finding a nice place on the lawn under a shade tree, spreading out a blanket, having a glass of Kool-aid and I was ready to start cutting out paper dolls. It was necessary to be very careful so as not to tear off a part of the doll or tabs on the clothes. That would have been devastating. There were clothes to cut out that were seasonal, snow paraphernalia, swimming outfits, ski gear, tennis suits, etc. Oh, what to cut out first!

If a person was very innovative, they could make more clothes by tracing around an outfit and designing it to their own liking. Of course, that would increase the dolls' wardrobe. If you happened to have a bridal gown in the collection, special care was given to carefully cut around all the trim while dreaming of the day when you would be a bride.

Sometimes a friend came over and shared costumes. Then it was more fun to pretend going skiing or swimming, or even planning a wedding.

If you weren't fortunate enough to have purchased paper dolls, or sometimes they wore out before your birthday, we'd take a catalog and cut out the models and wardrobe and have a whole family. You could even have furniture for a pretend home. One more use for an outdated catalog. Be sure not to take a current one.

I can remember my mother buying paper doll books for us when we went to Grandma Towner's as a means of quiet entertainment for the train ride and when we were at Grandma's. She was a dear lady but didn't take kindly to frivolity amid youngsters. Grandma's idea of entertainment was sitting on the front porch watching for the occasional car or two that go by all evening.

A girl in my class at BHS had a talent for drawing. She could make charming gowns and lovely faces and hair to match. I wonder if Marion Johnson ever put her talent to good use?

I'm wondering if some company would start producing paper doll books. Wouldn't little girls love a Princess Di collection or the McCauly septuplets? That could make a whole volume, or some of the Olympic gold medal winners.

I have a friend in Breckenridge, namely Phyllis Leshovsky, whom I believe still has some of her 1930s paper doll collection. We could spread out a blanket under a nice shade tree and instead of Kool-aid, we could have a carafe or coffee and try out all the different outfits. I'll never tell if we do!

Recently, I have seen paper dolls listed on auction sale billings. I'll bet they won't be 10 cents.

Honor Your Father on His Own June Day

*J*une is the month we celebrate Father's Day to honor our fathers, dads, pops, papas and whatever else we call them.

Picture this scene in your mind, Dad comes home from a hard day's work, his little girl runs to meet him with outstretched arms and a hug and kiss. A greeting like that has got to cure an Excedrin headache.

A father is someone who is willing to fix the chain on a bicycle, build a playhouse or listen to the trials of life in the day of a little girl.

There probably aren't too many dads who believe any man is good enough to marry his daughter. When the time comes, Dad walking his daughter down the aisle on her wedding day could generate a tear or two.

I remember my dad as being a big burly man. He was soft spoken and never laid a hand on us. I remember an instance where I had done something naughty, which by today's standards wouldn't have bee considered so bad, but mother still said, "wait until your dad gets home!" I was miserable all afternoon wondering what the punishment would be, which was punishment enough. The ordeal was forgotten, much to my relief.

Boys enjoy fishing and hunting trips with their dads. I don't think that too many dads turn down a request for money for the wheels to cruise up and down the street, or to see a favorite girlfriend.

I have a poem that is a good tribute to fathers, entitled "Your Name," written by Edgar A. Guest.

"You got it from your father, twas all he had to give. And right gladly he bestowed it. It's yours the while you live. You may lose the watch he gave you, and another you may claim, but remember, when tempted to be careful of his name.

"It was fair the day you got it, and a worthy name to bear, when he took it from his father, there was no dishonor there. Through the years he proudly wore it, to his father he was true, and that name was clean and spotless when he passed it on to you.

"Oh, there's so much he has given that he values not at all. He has watched you break your playthings in the days when you were small. You have lost the knife he gave you and you scattered many a games, but you'll never hurt your father if you're careful with his name.

"It's yours to wear forever, yours to wear while you live. Yours, perhaps, some distant morning, another boy to give. And you'll smile, as did your father, with a smile that all can share, of a clean and good name you are giving him to wear."

While I am having a cup of coffee, I'm thinking about how, as a child, I remember my dad's ability to drive a car. I thought it took a special talent. I remember him taking the blanket off the radiator, which was necessary to keep the radiator from freezing, and then cranking it to get the car going. It's no wonder there were few women drivers. I'm wondering how life would be today if we had to do all that just to drive away?

"May the Road Rise to Meet You" Irishmen

*S*t. Patrick's Day is a day for the Irish to show and display their heritage.

In the larger cities there are St. Patrick's Day Parades with the bag pipes and drum corps and Irish dancers. Any place you go there is an ample supply of green beer. Anyone who has an ounce of Irish in their blood qualifies to celebrate.

I'm 99 44/100 percent Irish, so corned beef and cabbage is a must on St. Patty's Day. I have tried to make my own and sometimes it's good and sometimes not. I think there is a technique to cooking corned beef that I haven't discovered. I'm thinking it has to cook slowly. If I make a full kettle, I have to eat it for a week—so I look for a place that has it on the menu.

Another Irish dish is slumgullian, a stew of something or everything.

I have an aunt, Rozine Finnegan Martin, who is a wonderfully typical Irish lady. She is a talented organist. A few years back at a Finnegan family reunion that I attended, she favored everyone with the favorite Irish tunes—"Danny Boy," "Mother McCree," "When Irish Eyes Are Smiling," "The Irish Wash Away Women," and "Who Threw the Overalls in Mrs. Murphy's Chowder?"

To hear an Irish tenor singing "Danny Boy" can curl you hair and put goose bumps all over your skin.

The Irish tend to be happy lot (as a rule). They like a good "Pat and Mike" joke, to which there are probably as many "Ole and Lena" jokes. Some are complementary and some not.

If you have an Irishman for a friend, you have a friend forever. But then you don't want to rub their fur the wrong way, either.

Irishmen are a good judge of character, as well as good musicians and will pursue anything to the end.

Ireland is noted for St. Patrick as their patron saint, the shamrock, Blarney Stone, leprechauns, and Irish potatoes. My mother used to tell me

I was full of blarney. Not being sure what it meant, I got my dictionary out to find out what I really was full of. Webster's version is a stone in Blarney Castle, County Cork, Ireland, said to impart skill in blarney to those who kiss it.

Blarney means to flatter, whiddle, coax. My oldest brother and his wife visited Ireland and I don't know if he kissed the Blarney Stone, but he must have gotten close.

There are a few Irish sayings; such as "Top O' the morning," "Begorrah," and "Erin go Bragh," (Ireland forever).

For all the Irish "wannabees," for this special day of St. Pat's, put an "O," "Mc," or "Mac" before your name and join us.

To everyone this Irish blessing:

"May the road rise up to meet you

May the wind be always at your back

May the sun shine warm upon your face

And rain fall soft upon your field,

And until we meet again,

May God hold you in the palm of his hand."

"Erin go bragh!"

I think I'll hunt me up a leprechaun and see if I can find that pot o' gold at the end of my rainbow.

New Computer will Turn Even Winter into an Enjoyable Season

Computer mania has hit me over the head like a 2-by-4. I had never thought I wanted a computer. They're fine if you have one. But me, having a computer?

In the first place, computers are costly. At my age, what would I want with one except to do my stories, which I could probably hand write-faster. Also, since I have limited space, where would I put it? With all this to think about—forget it!

One day last month my sister Gayle called and asked if I wanted a computer. "Yes! I'll take it!" Instant solitaire. I'm sure I can learn that much. It might take me a month, but I'll do it.

I even invested in a computer desk and sent the old one out to my son's.

As soon as I got the desk, Gayle and her husband, Doug, came and set the computer up for me. With about a half-hour of instruction, they had to leave. I sat there and looked at the monstrosity and decided to take a chance. I did get solitaire on the screen, to my amazement.

It didn't take long before I had things boggled real well. My 7-year-old grandson, Adam, came for the day and I told him that I boo-booed the computer. He turned the machine on and rectified the situation with no problem. To think that I had reservations about even letting him turn it on.

"Remember, Grandma, this is how you do it," Adam said.

He thought I should learn the paintbrush program so he brought it up on screen. When it comes to drawing I will never be a Grandma Moses. I decided to give it a try, as long as it was something simple like a barn. Adam said he would do the fence and that I would do the rest.

He gave me a blow-by-blow description of how to do it.

Adam did such a good job of instructing, I felt like I was back in school. The idea of me painting a computer picture at my age…why, I felt like a first grader with my first art project.

The printer was giving us some trouble, so we had to get our neighbor Julie to help us. I guess I would have to say everything I learned about the computer, I learned from a 7-year-old.

In a week's time, I am pretty adept with it. My other grandson, Aaron, made a comment about my "hunt and peck system." I did learn to type on an Underwood typewriter, you know. Just think, it probably won't be much longer before kids ask, "what's a typewriter?"

This computer is amazing. It even has a pullout drawer with a cover for my coffee. Now if I can print this on the printer without losing it, I will be amazed. There, I did it.

I have been dreading winter, but I think my computer and I will enjoy it. My nights are shorter now and the meals are often burnt offerings.

The Pledge of Allegiance

I pledge allegiance to the flag of the United States of America, and to the republic for which it stands, one nation, under God, indivisible, with liberty and justice for all.

June 14 is Flag Day. When we recite the Pledge of Allegiance, what are we thinking? Are we just reciting words or do we realize what a tremendous statement it is? Webster's Dictionary has many versions of the word "pledge." It is a promise or agreement. "Allegiance" is the duty of being loyal to one's ruler or government or country.

In essence, in the first line we make a promise to be loyal to our country, and to a republic that is a state or nation, in which supreme power rests.

"One nation under God" is quite self-explanatory. "Indivisible" is that which cannot be divided, with liberty—freedom or release from slavery, imprisonment, captivity or any other form of arbitrary control. "Justice" is the use of authority and power to uphold what is right or just.

With changing times, liberty and justice have taken on a whole new meaning in respect to humanity.

There have been many songs written about our flag. In "The Star Spangled Banner," the first and fourth stanzas were written by Francis Scott Key in 1871, and Congress adopted the song in 1931 as our

National Anthem, not to forget the March King, John Phillip Sousa's "Stars and Stripes Forever," or Lee Greenwood's "God Bless the USA."

In my early childhood, in school, I learned a poem that went like this:

See our big flag
Up, up she goes
Red as a rose
Blue as the sky
Long may she fly.

I had for some reason associated our flag's birthday as July 4th, but while looking at my "Stars and Stripes" etiquette book, the first flag as unfurled by President Washington, January 2, 1776. July 4 is the day to add a new star for the admission of a new state.

The flag is very much a part of our daily lives. We should always respect it because it represents everything we are as Americans—everything we hope to be. The latter paragraph was taken from "Etiquette of the Stars and Stripes" by the Veterans of Foreign Wars.

While we sip our coffee, let's look up the meaning of respect. When I look down the street at the sight of flags on every street corner we can fully appreciate one nation under God, indivisible, with liberty and justice for all. It tells visitors we are dedicated Americans.

Thank Veterans for Their Part in Keeping All Americans Free

*T*his past century has seen numerous wars. Veterans Day is a day set aside to honor our nation's veterans from all those wars and is celebrated Nov. 11.

This century has seen World War I, World War II, the Korean Conflict, The Vietnam War, and in later years Desert Storm in the Mideast, among others.

Wars have always had the pros and cons as to necessity. So far, the conflicts have kept us free. But what is freedom? Webster's Dictionary states "freedom" as a state or equality of being free, especially exemption or liberation from the control of some person or arbitrary power."

Without the sacrifices of our veterans, we wouldn't have freedoms to enjoy—freedom of speech, freedom from want, freedom of press. The word freedom is often exchanged with liberty, which is described as a right, an area, where privileges prevail.

Our veterans didn't always have a choice. There was the draft during World War II. If your number came up it was mandatory to go, although there were deferments for farm labor, a chronic illness or a job that contributed to the war effort.

Today, young men must register when they're 18. However, it is a choice to go or not.

We owe a special gratitude to our veterans for their sacrifices and to their families. As the mother of two Servicemen, I can relate to the daily things that run through a mother's mind.

Our veteran's hospitals are filled with men who have come home limbless and hospitalized with countless results from the atrocities of war, not to forget the men and women who came home with memories of scenes that remain with them and often return to remind them.

Our veterans deserve every privilege available. Without them, where would our liberty, freedom and privileges be? My heart aches for the families of the men and women who didn't come home safely.

Veterans Day keeps them alive in our hearts. They aren't, and won't be forgotten as long as freedom allows us the liberty and freedom to have a Veterans Day. We need to give thanks for the freedoms because so often they have been threatened and we have come close to losing them. God has truly blessed America when we hear of the atrocities of Kosovo. Have you ever pictured yourself in one of those camps?

Our veterans are the heroes of this past century and deserve all due respect. Here is a poem from the Minneapolis Tribune during the World War II era that is fitting. You might have a cup of coffee while reading it, and maybe have a tissue close at hand.

Conversion

By Frances Angermayer

Look God, I have never spoken to you—
But now—I want to say "how do you do?"
You see, God, they told me you didn't exist—
And like a fool—I believed all of this.
Last night from a shell hole I saw your sky—
I figured right then they had told me a lie.
Had I taken time to see the things you made,
I'd know they weren't calling a spade a spade.
I wonder, God, if you'd shake my hand
Somehow—I feel that you will understand.
Funny—I had to come to this hellish place,
Before I had the time to see your face.
Well, I guess there isn't much more to say,
But I'm sure glad, God, I met you today.
I guess the "zero hour" will soon be here,
But I'm not afraid since I know you're here,
The signal!—Well God—I'll have to go.
I like you lots—this I want you to know—
Look, now—this will be a horrible right—
Who knows—I may come to your house tonight—
Though I wasn't friendly with you before,
I wonder, God—if you'd wait at your door—
Look—I'm crying! Me—Shedding tears!—
I wish I'd known you these many years—

Well, I have to go now, God—Goodbye.
Strange—Since I met you—I'm not afraid to die.

Patriot Songs Suddenly Pop Up
with Advent of World War

I turn the radio on first thing in the morning. Often, there will be a song new to the listening audience. Music today is so different than in "Our Century Past." Then, music was soft and the words meaningful. Today, it's loud and colorful.

What I really want to evaluate is the number of patriotic songs that are composed as compared to pop tunes. It seems that a war will bring out a new patriot song or two.

For instance, World War I claims, "When Johnny Comes Marching Home," and "Just Before the Battle Mother." World War I songs were more dedicated to the foot soldier. There are probably a few more songs that I can't remember.

World War II gave us, "There's a Star Spangled Banner Waving Somewhere," George Cohan's "Yankee Doodle Dandy," "American Patrol," and "Any Bonds Today?" This song promoted the sale of savings bonds. There also was "This Is My Country," and Fred Waring's spectacular arrangement of "Battle Hymn of the Republic." Remember back to "Coming In On a Wing and a Prayer"? The Andrews Sisters are remembered for entertaining at USO's with "Boogie Woogie Bugle Boy."

We have our old standards, like "The Star Spangled Banner," "America," and "America the Beautiful."

John Phillip Sousa composed many marches dedicated to America like, "Under the Double Eagle" and "Stars and Stripes Forever," which would get a No. 1 rating with me. There also was "National Emblem," "Washington Post," and "Semper Fidelis."

Lee Greenwood's "God Bless the USA" became popular during Desert Storm.

When you compare the number of patriotic songs to the non-patriotic versions, I would guess the patriotic ones are outnumbered.

There are other songs not mentioned here, to make a long story short.

It is said that music creates unity, no matter what your age or era of music.

I have a question. Why do we have to be involved in a war to have a patriotic song composed? Perhaps for the memory? Something to think about, "Our Century Past," over a cup of coffee.

Armed Forces Day & National Bird

*M*ay is the month we reflect on a couple of things, such as the fact that Mother's Day is set aside to honor our mothers. No matter how small the gift, mothers will love the gift and the giver. It's always good for a hug and kiss or two.

The other day to reflect upon is Memorial Day. Remembering as far back as I've lived here, Hankinson has recognized Memorial Day. Those years we even had a parade. The American Legion color guard and arms, the high school band, Boy Scouts and Girl Scouts, if there were a troop, would participate.

I admire the American Legion and VFW's as they honor our war veterans on Memorial Day. They honor the deceased veterans with our national flag, gun salutes and taps.

It is heart-warming to families when these men pay their tribute at a funeral, no matter how cold. They're there during windy, wintry weather or through the heat of summer. They give of themselves as they did for our great country. Thank you. The flags are waving for you.

Now that I'm off my soapbox, I would like to suggest, since May has a national holiday, to take a look at our national bird—the Bald Eagle. He doesn't get a lot of attention and I thought he deserved some merit.

Are you a bird watcher? No? Well, neither am I. Oh, I do enjoy seeing a lovely bird flitting around my yard. But how many of us have had the joy of seeing a real American eagle? Actually, the American eagle isn't the most colorful bird in our country. I haven't seen a real eagle, only ceramic ones, or pictures, and television scenes of eagles soaring.

I remember hearing that at one time the turkey was chosen as our national bird. Oh, yes, the turkey is a proud bird but usually is the main entree at Thanksgiving dinner.

Let's take a look at our national bird. He looks so regal. Looking at him perched on a limb, how he holds his head so high. He is a proud bird. Look at him as he soars through the beautiful blue sky. The wing span magnificently spanned out and looking as if he is saying, "I'm looking at a country of people strong in their beliefs of God, country and all it stands for. I have a lot to be proud of.

You know, it's easy to see why the eagle was chosen to represent our country. He stands for all the things we are proud of—the American flag, Statue of Liberty, Armed Forces, freedom, and love of God.

Eagle, you were a great choice!

Remember that May 19 is Armed Forces Day. We appreciate you, the men and women serving our country.

World War II Rations

As a teenager at the time of World War II, everybody was issued ration books because items needed for the war effort had to be conserved at home. I happened to be looking through an old photo album and found some ration stamps for gas. If I remember correctly, the household had to report family members count to the ration board and depending on the size of the family, stamps were issued accordingly. I believe the larger the family the more stamps received.

Some of the items that were on the ration list were gasoline, so driving was limited to only necessary trips, thus vacation trips were not across the country treks. Sugar was another item I remember as being scarce. Today, if I want to bake a cake or cookies, I don't have to wonder if I should spare the sugar, but can you imagine being limited to the amount you could use. I'm sure cookies were rationed to two and not a handful. Often, syrup, honey or molasses were substituted.

Shoes were also rationed. I would guess there were a lot of bare footed people.

Oh, yes, then there was meat rationing. At the store, the meat counters had a very slim choice to offer. I recall one incident where my mother had asked me if I would go up town and get some meat. I was quite proud to be chosen to do the job. Because of the rationing it was important to do it wisely and economically. I proceeded to walk to the store and very intent on doing a good job proceeded to the meat counter. To my surprise I found it bare except for kidneys. Well, my mother would sure know how to prepare kidneys. Moms know everything. I bought 6 kidneys, without choice and proceeded on my way home with my cherished purchase. I, pleased with my purchase, presented my parcel to mom, and she had what I assumed was a look of pleasure, but it didn't take long to change my opinion that it was a look of, "What do you do with these things?" I'm sure there are numerous people in the world that could make a delicacy of kidneys, but not in our household. We decided as an alternative to garbage pailing them, we would scan the recipe books. There just might be a delicious formula to whet the appetite. At last, a recipe for kidney stew. It went something like this. Stew the kidneys and add raw potatoes in chunks, etc. During the cooking process we decided it was necessary to open the doors, then the windows. We had a family council meeting to decide if this delicacy should be smothered with onions and garlic, but the alternative to let the dog enjoy our entree won by majority.

I don't remember what we substituted our meal with—most likely the good ol' standby—eggs.

Lard was another item that was used sparingly. It was strained through a filter, especially made for lard and reused.

Tires made of rubber were also a scarce item.

How would we cope with all this today? There was no choice. You just made do and as good Americans we did it.

I didn't have to worry about meat shopping for a long time.

Statue of Liberty

*J*uly is the month of hot weather, picnics, vacations, swimming, golfing and Independence Day. A good time for reflecting on the U.S. flag and Statue of Liberty.

The flag is very much a part of our daily lives. We should respect the flag because it represents everything we, as Americans, are and everything we hope to be.

Let's think on what our flag would say to us if it could:

Here you are sitting on the front porch in your favorite rocking chair. The flag is overhead wafting in the soft breeze. It might say, "Good morning, Ben. That was a nice rain we had last night. You're looking well this morning.

'You know, you and I have seen a lot of changes over the years. The horseless carriage, airplanes, electricity, space age, computers, and many wars. It makes me proud that I grace government building and schools. In church I stand by the Christian flag and hear refrains from "God Bless

America," "Battle Hymn of the Republic," or my favorite "The Star Spangled Banner."

'Look! There is a parade coming down the street. I'm leading the parade. The people are saluting. Parades are so much fun with the marching bands, clowns, and so many floats.

'Have you noticed, looking down the street, that there is a flag on every corner and see how the homes display me? If we could go to the cemetery, we would see many flags on the graves of those who served our country. Some gave their lives at a very young age, and some lived out their lives to a good age. It makes me proud to be part of them.

'Ben, you look like you could use a cup of coffee. I'll just wave at the people as they go by." Ben has listened attentively and adds, "I had a letter from an old friend of yours. Listen while I read it to you:"

'Dear Friends, I am Miss Liberty—properly known as "Liberty Enlightening the World." My address is Ellis Island. I stand tall, proud and with dignity. Yes, I am in my golden years and feeling my age, but so with age goes wisdom. I would love to have you come and sit around me and tell you stories of the changes I have seen from freedom of slavery to the present day women's rights. How about a story about the early immigrants coming over on storm tossed boats to seek out our land of opportunity and freedom. They look at me and smile with a love I couldn't refuse.

"My middle name 'Enlighten' that means to free from ignorance, prejudice of or superstition, also to inform. Oh, what a warm feeling to know I stand for these things for my people. You know, I have seen shiploads of service men come home and they look at me with great pride. I can feel them saying, 'We did it for you!' I ask, 'Where are your brothers?' They lower their heads and humbly reply, 'God has taken them home. But their mission has not been forgotten. It is because of them that we are here.' My reply, 'I salute you with my lighted torch—you the living and the families of those who didn't come home.'

'Would you believe I have a few namesakes? Remember the Liberty Bell? The Bell of Independence Hall? Just about as old as I am. We might even have the same birthday. There have even been ships named for me. Oh! It does make me proud to light the way for ships.

Have a happy birthday, Miss Liberty. We do have a lot in common.

While you are packing your July 4th picnic, be sure there is plenty of Kool-Aid, coffee and wouldn't homemade ice cream be good!

The Advancement of the Plane

*T*his year we hear about "Our Century Past." I have seen only part of the century so it took some looking into history to relate to the first part.

One thing that comes to mind is what our century would have been like without the airplane. It was December 17, 1903 when Wilber and Orville Wright had worked so diligently to perfect the airplane in order to make their first successful flight to Kittyhawk, North Carolina.

It was in the 1890s that the Wright Brothers became interested in flying machines; however flying machines date back to 300-400 BC. Back in 1500 BC Leonardo de Vinci drew plans for a flying machine with flapping wings.

It is amazing how the airplane has progressed from the 2 wing propelled machine to the Transoceanic commercial planes. The advancements in airplane technology have been rapid since the 40s. How much faster is it to get on a plane to visit relatives or a business venture than driving a vehicle for days besides the overnight stays on the way by car? Mail being transported by plane has to be an improvement over pony express or stagecoach. Crop spraying is a quicker mode than by tractor.

Military airplanes are the biggest advancement when you think of what was used in World War I. Most planes could only fly 60 to 70 miles per hour. Great strides were made in airplane advancement at the time of

World War II. Planes could carry twice as heavy a load and travel twice as fast.

When we see all the changes that have taken place form the Wright Brother's propeller to the Stealth Bombers it is really awesome.

With all these rapid changes—has this made us a better world? I wonder what the Wright Brother's would be thinking if they would see or know what their invention has produced?

Something to think about, "Our Century Past," over a cup of coffee.

Hankinson could be the City of Pine Trees

*O*ccasionally, I take it upon myself to go for a short walk. In the fall, the trees are so lovely with their leaves turning colors.

Have you really looked at the different trees, seeing how the shapes of their leaves differ? The colors are so vibrant, from a deep red to bright yellow, orange and shades of brown and gold.

As long as I can remember, kids have had to bring leaf specimens to school to identify both the leaf and tree it came from. I think this is still an important part of science.

Years ago, the leaves were sorted and classified. This was by no means the end of the leaf. They served a dual purpose, such as Friday's art class when students picked a shapely leaf, pinned it on a paper and spatter painted it with a screen and toothbrush.

After it was dry, you removed the leaf and had a very nice picture.

I have recently noticed the number of evergreens in town. I counted 36 along a two-block area west of my house in Hankinson. Evergreens stand so stately and tall. If you look out a second-story window, you can still look high enough to see the top. They aren't the kind of tree you can sit under for shade, as usually the branches are quite close to the ground. Some evergreens produce acorns that can be used decoratively, though.

There are two evergreens in my yard I though were nuisances because they blocked my view. I found out they are an arborvitae tree that is unusual around here. After learning this bit of information they became quite lovely.

Most evergreens are the needle variety, but the in my yard are more lacey.

While driving around town, take notice of the number of evergreens on both sides of town. I counted as many as 10 in one yard. It would be interesting to know how old they are and if they were planted when Hankinson had a nursery west of town. We could be known as the *City of Pine Trees* or *City of Evergreens.*

Something to ponder about over a cup of coffee. Just think, if there were a star on top of each tree for Christmas how bright the night would be.

Unusual Sports

I'm going to digress from my usual tales of the old days and tell about my vacation, which proved to be very different from my usual trip to Detroit Lakes to visit my mother. (Well, I did visit her, and went to Crazy Days, and then went home and cleaned house for the rest of it.)

This summer I learned to enjoy two sports, which are uncommon in our town, but if you travel a few miles, you can enjoy these fun sports.

I've found that soccer and car racing are very enjoyable.

Earlier this summer my oldest son, Paul, who lives in Elk River, Minnesota, called and said he would be coming to visit. He invited me to go to Moorhead to the VFW-sponsored soccer games to watch his daughter, Karen, play.

I quickly said I would go, but had some after thoughts that what I knew about soccer you could hold on the end of a toothpick. *"I'll be bored* to tears, I thought. *If I don't like it, what will I do all day there? Too far from shopping centers! Oh, well, Granny will be a good sport and go learn something new."*

We got there and set up our chairs and got my soccer hat on and got comfy for the first hour and a half game. It didn't take long to catch on to what a foul was and how a goal was scored.

At my age, I won't try soccer. The way they kick that ball with their ankles, I wouldn't be able to walk for a week, or more.

I couldn't believe the way they hit the ball with their heads—I guess you can't touch the ball with your hands. I would have skull cramps for two weeks with just one hit—or be laid out on the field. And, if you accidentally kicked the ball into the opponent's goal or over the net, the penance would be one push-up.

Soccer is a fast-moving game and when you kick the ball it will more than likely go to an opponent. The ball is not as easily controlled as it is in basketball.

In the Elk River area, they hire professional soccer players from England to coach the teams. Unaware of this, I heard these British accents and wondered if English teams were here.

It seems you need ambition to play soccer. It's no game for a piker. Keep playing, Karen! I'll keep going and enjoying as a spectator.

Another part of my sporting vacation was spent "in the pits." The racing pits that is.

My daughter, Jane, came from Bismarck and took me shopping in Detroit Lakes. While we were shopping, she had found a pair of white coveralls. "You have to wear a pair of white coveralls to be a lab technician?" I asked. No, no, mom. I have to have white coveralls to work the pits.

Mama mia! My size 8 daughter, my petite daughter, the one it took all our smarts to raise her…a pit man, uh…woman…pit person?

Oh, well, good for you if it's your cup of tea to fix flats, work on hot engines and fix bent tin. It's not mine, and it really didn't turn my crank until that day during this summer's vacation.

After a day of mall shopping and rummage sale-ing, my daughter announced that we had to hurry home and get supper going because we would be going to the car races in Mandan.

When I left Hankinson I knew we would be shopping a day or so, but me going to car races? Unthought of. Never! But once more I decided I could be just as bored there as sitting home by myself, because the Friday night races are No. 1 if your priority list bottom is No. 10.

"C'mon, mom! Eat faster! We have to be there by 6:30 to get a good seat," she says.

I'm still chewing on the way. I thought, "What's the hurry? There might be 50 people there—a good Hankinson crowd."

We climbed to the top of the bleachers, which were already full. Getting to the top wasn't bad, but I worried through the whole thing how I would get down after sitting for four hours.

After we sat for half an hour, the racecars started going around the track slowly. I thought that if this is a race, I could *run* that fast. Little did I realize they were "packing the track" after numerous waterings in preparation for the race.

Before the race started, a young gal sang a rendition of "The Star Spangled Banner," beautifully done.

When the cars lined up and made their yellow flag (slow) warm-up lap, the roar of the engines was so deafening I thought my eardrums would blow, but that was nothing compared to the noise when the green flag (go) was dropped. I thought the top of my head would fly off.

After awhile I became accustomed to it. The crowd was wonderfully sympathetic. If a racer had a boo boo or there was a three or four-car entanglement, the first concern was for the safety of the driver.

I learned the yellow flag means slow down, the white means one lap to go, and the checkered flag is for the winner.

Aside from the hair-raising pileups, it was a fun evening, and I even picked up a copy of *Inside Track*, the auto racing newspaper published two blocks from my house by *Hankinson News* Publisher Gary Nelson.

After a race or two, I can carry on a conversation with Gary about Streets, Late Models, Wissota Modifieds, and "packing the track."

I have a lot of respect for the drivers. Each car is set up to certain standards, and much TLC is given to the cars, and the policy is strictly, "Safety First."

When the cars are set up bumper-to-bumper and side-by-side, my first thought was that if I was driving the car beside or in front I would have a fender bender before the green flag. The drivers have to be alert and concentrate fully on what they are doing. I told my daughter they couldn't pay me enough to get in one of those cars.

Her reply was, "I'd sit by Richard Petty any time.

Jane and Mitch were racing fans when they lived in Lisbon, as they had access to a racetrack there. I never really took it seriously until we drove up to their home one day last year and there sat a car for this year's races. I didn't realize that I would be a race car mother-in-law fan.

See! I have gone to the pits.

Crazy Geese Fly in a T-Formation and Score is what You do to a Ham, Right?

*A*ccomplishing new ventures has all of a sudden become important to me. For instance, this last year of our century, I learned the basics of the computer. I'll probably never master it, but I know enough to enjoy it.

My goal for this year will be to learn football terminology. All through high school I went to games. Our three boys played football and now I go to watch the local football games and I still don't understand all of the terminology.

To make football more enjoyable for people like me who don't understand it, I made up a glossary of terms for references:

1. Touchdown—what UFO's do.
2. Sack—sack of what?
3. Safety zone—what you look for when driving down the highway.
4. Marker—what you address packages with.
5. Receiving back—the complaint department after Christmas.
6. Tight end—a great derriere.
7. Recover—what you do at night when you kick the covers off.
8. Hail Mary—a Catholic prayer.
9. Flag—something you salute or wave.
10. T-Formation—How crazy, mixed up geese fly.
11. Goal—attained aspirations.
12. Score—what you do to a ham.
13. Defense—defeat of deduck went over defense before detail.
14. Offense—something happens when sitting on it.
15. Penalty—what you get for speeding.
16. Illegal—sick bird.
17. Wings—what an angel needs to land on our shoulder.
18. Conversion—changing habits.
19. Linebacker—holds up the clothes line ropes.
20. Sideline—an extra job to supplement the income.
21. Win—might happen at the casino.

22. Loss—something you put in a special place and isn't there when you look for it.
23. Coach—what Cinderella rode in.
24. Kick off—what you do with your shoes after a hard day.
25. Block—toy for a child.
26. Tackle—something used for fishing.
27. Time out—a corner for the unruly.
28. Punt—what you do after a 65-yard run.
29. Turnover—piecrust with filling or what you do when it's time to get up.
30. Kick—what you get out of an Ole and Lena story.
31. Nose guard—what you put on your dog so he won't bite you.

There are probably more terms with which I'm not familiar. Anyway, this bit of nonsense may make watching football more enjoyable or listening to sportscasts less tedious. While I have a cup of coffee, I will try to think of something intelligent to accomplish in the new millennium. Happy New Year!

The Waiting Game

I'm going to be a Great Grandma soon for the first time by my only Granddaughter and her husband. I've been a Mom and Grandma—but Great Grandma? I was elated when I heard the news and after mulling it over in my mind I thought that makes me 4 generations old!

When I think about it being a Mom 50 years ago was so different than being a Mom today. I wonder if you can even buy diaper material anymore? Diapers were bought by the yard; cut, sewed and hemmed by machine. After washing they were taken to the clothes line, hung to dry (not thrown in a drier) brought in, folded and put away. Baby bottles had to be washed, sterilized, and formula made every morning. Most babies were raised on a formula of boiled milk and boiled water with Karo syrup. Heaven help you if you walked away from the stove, it was sure to boil over.

Today babies come with instructions, parenting classes, instruction books, prepared formula, and throw away diapers. I recall my first attempt at putting on a disposable diaper. I don't know who was more exasperated, me or the child. The tape stuck to my fingers but not the diaper or the tape tore lose and finally—enough. I got out the old stand-by safety pins.

I haven't seen any books about how to be a Great Grandma. What would it include? I thin the biggest necessity would be a rocking chair. No, not the soft cushy kind but one with wooden rockers that when you rock the chair eventually ends up by the door. I gave Paul the rocking chair that his Grandpa rocked him in so that now he will be able to rock his Grandchild. This rocking chair will have rocked 5 generations of babies and is probably good for a few more. If I were to write a book on how to be a Great Grandparent I think all it would contain would be 2 necessary things, a good rocker and a lot of TLC. It sure wouldn't be a best seller, but what more do we need? What more could a Baby want from a Great Grandparent besides the other necessities?

This spring my time has been consumed with crocheting little things. Sweaters, cowboy bootees, afghans, etc. It's so much fun.

Pretty soon, while I wait for the mail and have my coffee, I can look for pictures in the mail. Who needs a book anyway?

Girls are as Scarce as Hen's Teeth

IT'S A GIRL!!! Finally I'm a Great Grandma, and to a girl! Girls tend to be a phenomenon in our immediate family.

Starting with Alvina Medenwaldt Buck, born in 1878. She had eight brothers. Can you imagine life being brought up with eight brothers? I had two, one four years older and one fourteen years younger. The younger one was no threat but the older one offered competition when it came to sibling scraps. It was always good for running to Mommy for some relished sympathy. The—he did—she did—he did thing.

Alvina, who was the mother of Clemens Buck and grandmother of Janice Medenwaldt, Diane Milbrandt and Mervin Buck, and our daughter, Jane, were the only two girls raised on the Medenwaldt farm along with seventeen boys in one hundred twelve years, the nineteenth and twentieth centuries.

My granddaughter informed me that Kayla's picture was on the computer. I ran across the alley to Julie and gave her the .com address and she brought up the computer picture of her so I had and instant color picture of her less than two days old. The wonders of modern miracles. For eight years Karen, Paul's daughter, has been queen bee and family princess, so move over mom, you can be queen bee but Kayla is the princess.

It probably isn't terribly ironic of only four girls in three centuries. There are probably generations of all bys or all girls. I'll say this is interesting.

While I'm having my coffee, I'm wondering if there is something in the water at the farm that is causing the scarcity of girls in the relation?

Jean recently put new upholstery on my rocking chair so I'm ready for a visit from Kayla. She also took the squeak out of it. I also have the TLC and safety pins in case the tapes get stuck to my fingers.

Fitting Pieces of the Puzzle Together Fills the Days

*N*eedless to reiterate that January and February are L-O-N-G months. What—with the snow, cold and ice, trips uptown are minimal.

Cabin fever sets in when you are in a home that only requires 10 steps from one room to the other. I learned that along with my usual daily necessities and hobbies, time becomes long. I have taken a liking to picture puzzles. They are a good pastime and tend to become addictive. I find myself inching over to the puzzle to put in a piece, and before I know it, I'm making myself comfortable and putting in one more piece and another until all of a sudden, an hour has sneaked by.

Once in awhile, it dawns on me I should be doing something of more importance and I could hang a guilt trip on myself real easy by putting in a piece or two more. A person can spend days putting a puzzle together and then you break it apart and put it back in the box. I don't like putting a puzzle together a second time, so I have found some neighbors who like puzzles, also, and can readily make a trade.

Puzzles can be challenging, especially when there are few colors or lots of colors in a small area. The 3-D puzzles, I've heard, can be quite difficult but are beautiful when done.

Puzzles are a good pastime. In retrospect, the fact you can work on them anytime and then leave them works well for me. It isn't something that you pick up and put away. Right now, mine is cluttering half the table. You think you have a piece that for sure will fit in a certain spot and proves you wrong thus testing your patience. When you get to the end of the puzzle and there are four holes and three pieces left you frantically look, to no avail—then try the floor.

While I have a cup of coffee, I can put in a few more pieces and puzzle over what I will have for lunch. It probably should be something that doesn't have to be cooked.

Bird Feeding—Fun but Costly

*B*ird watching can be fun. My neighbor across the street, Ruth Krump, has an envious backyard. When it comes to being a nice backyard, mine has much to be desired, so I thought a birdhouse or two might attract some feathered friends.

A while back my son Paul and his wife Kay were here. Upon their arrival, they brought a large box into the house. In the box were several bird feeders. They put them outside on hangers. Paul and Kay also had brought a quantity of bird feed.

The first day was uneventful. No birds had found the feeders. By the second day, they were starting to appear: three goldfinches at once and a woodpecker tapping on the suet bar rhythmically. The sparrows and wrens are now numerous and there are lots of grayish birds with red heads and breasts. The crows make an occasional appearance, as well as the doves. The humming birds haven't been around yet. They usually make a pit stop in May and don't come back until August. Humming birds are interesting to watch, especially when they become feisty.

The suet bars seem to be the favorite choice over the seeds for my birds. It's so popular that the birds dive bomb at the suet cage. If it's occupied, only then they will go to the feeders. The way the bird feed is diminishing, I'm glad for the supply I've got.

There's a bird out there that isn't very happy with the cuisine. He keeps spitting it out.

The way birds eat at the suet bars; they apparently don't have to be concerned with cholesterol.

I may have to invest in a bird book. We don't seem to have the varied species here that are in areas a bit further south.

These birds are fed quite well. However, they don't like my car for some reason. I have moved it to different locations, to no avail. Maybe it's the color or model. If they continue leaving their presents, I may cut their rations.

For now, I'll just sit at the table with my coffee and enjoy the birds. I've decided the benefits outweigh the hazards. Summer *is* for the birds.

Battle of the Elements

*E*very once in a while my furnace has a thing about liking to put me in a panic. This time of year not so much, although there are days that are damp and taking the chill off the house makes it more comfy. Occasionally, if it hasn't been on for a few weeks, it doesn't want to start right away, so I have to call Jim to push the reset button and then it goes. I do get frustrated with it and sometimes I think a good swift kick might straighten it out.

But then there is the alternative. A wood/coal furnace. Wood heat actually is more comfortable—even heat all the time. When I think of using wood, getting it in, or coal, keeping it going all night in the winter, taking out ashes and invariably there would be a pile on the floor, chimney fires, cleaning and polishing stovepipes. I really don't know where I would pile wood. My house runeth over.

A furnace does have its good qualities. Not having to be tended and stoked at night, coming into a night warm house after being out in the cold.

Sometimes if the wind was in a direction not to accommodate the chimney the stove would emit smoke into the house.

Electric heaters aren't much consolation, especially if the power is off. They only heat where they sit. If you have a kerosene heater you need ventilation, thus defeating the purpose.

Electric heat would be a nice even heat and probably eliminate one of my unfavorite tasks of dusting. Recently I saw a sign stating "You can touch my dust, but don't write your name in it."

Should the power be off in the winter, a furnace wouldn't heat because the blowers wouldn't go. Electric heat wouldn't work, so back to the old wood/coal furnace.

Bible Thumping

*T*hursday morning is a given fact that it is devotions day at the nursing home. Several local ladies and myself go the St. Gerard's and spend a while doing devotions with the protestant elderly. We do a Bible reading, opening and closing prayer, a psalm and sing several hymns.

We try to sing seasonal songs and they especially enjoy the old standards. Some of the old standards they enjoy are "The Old Rugged Cross," "Rock of Ages," "Onward Christian Soldiers," "Stand Up, Stand Up for Jesus," "What a Friend We have in Jesus," and "Jesus Loves Me, This I Know." We have the large print hymnals to accommodate the failing eyesight. Some are still not able to read the words and yet is so amazing how well they know the words from memory. Sometimes they request a favorite song so we do that too. Sometimes the 2nd and 3rd verses of a song fail the memory but they join in for the chorus. One lady often reminds us that she learned that song in school.

The Thursday morning devotions were started many years ago by Mary Bottihen, herself now a resident of Dakota Estates. It is said, "Politics and religion are two things to stay away from in conversation." I don't know how well Mary is versed in politics, but the Bible is her forte.

We have a piano and organ for our singing. They seem to prefer to sing to the organ; maybe it gives more of a church aire. Lucia and Viola are wonderful singers. Try as I will, I can't out-sing then; but then God hears all the birds.

After devotions we treat ourselves to coffee at Rosie's Bakery. We are the Thursday morning "Bible Thumpers."

Birthdays Can Be Fun

*R*ecently I had my 35th birthday for the second time. I've been trying to ignore it, but my sister Gayle suggested we should do something for my birthday. My first thought was I'll have to clean off the dining room table. Don't make me do it. I'd almost rather not celebrate the day.

I'm wondering if a lot of people have a table like mine? Right now there is a place to eat, a Halloween place mat for Adam, my book manuscript and the junk mail which consists of 'should I garbage or save?' I'll think about it, so through the seek it accumulates. If I didn't have junk mail, I wouldn't have garbage.

Recently I was at my daughter-in-law Laurie's, and her kitchen table was so neat and pretty, so I'm questioning myself as to why I can't do that? I commented on how nice her table looked. When I was ready to go out the door she said, "Don't look in the writing desk." They have an elderly roll top desk. Wonderful for putting the junk mail in and rolling down the cover. What could I throw out to put in a desk? Nothing, so my table will have to suffice.

One of my favorite birthday presents was when Jim & Laurie took me to Fargo for dinner and then to the Fargo Dome to watch the Hankinson Pirates win the Region 1 football title. Before we went home we did some shopping and supper. I enjoyed the day so much.

I'll see if I can make room on my table for a cup of coffee and decide what to garbage and what to keep.

ABOUT THE AUTHOR

The Author was born in Morris, Minnesota. Raised in the Breckenridge, Minnesota-Wahpeton, North Dakota area. After marriage, husband Eldon and herself lived on a now 6 generation, century farm north of Hakinson, North Dakota. They had 3 sons and 1 daughter. The second son, Edmund, and daughter, Jane, passed away in adulthood. Her oldest son, Paul, lives in Monticello, Minnesota, and youngest son, Jim, lives on the home farm where she was inspired to write about heritage having lived with most of the items referred to.

www.ingramcontent.com/pod-product-compliance
Lightning Source LLC
Chambersburg PA
CBHW020251290526
45784CB00003B/1202